HEATING YOUR CHURCH

William Bordass

and

Colin Bemrose

CHURCH HOUSE PUBLISHING
Church House, Great Smith Street, London SW1P 3NZ

ISBN 0 7151 7570 X

Published 1996 for the Council for the Care of Churches by Church House Publishing

© Central Board of Finance of the Church of England 1996

Printed in England by the Longdunn Press Ltd, Bristol

Contents

Illustrations and Tables

Introduction

Ever since churches first started installing heating, the subject has been one of debate and has needed expert advice. Heating methods, fuels and personal expectations have all changed since then, but the objective remains to improve personal comfort whilst preserving the building.

There are two main aims for this book. First, to act as a reference work: each church is unique and there are no universal solutions. Heating needs depend not only on the church's structure but its location, condition, contents, present heating, usage, the expectations of the congregation and the finance available. Secondly: to assist the decision-making process when changes to heating are being contemplated or when considering systems for a new church or ancillary buildings.

Rarely can one make a simple and unambiguous decision about heating. Inevitably the system chosen will have an impact on the building, what it contains and the people who use it. Each will respond in different ways, and compromises are virtually inevitable.

Churches are living entities, for worship and mission. Internal conditions need to help fulfil these purposes. At the end of the twentieth century this often means aiming for higher levels of personal comfort than was the norm one hundred, or even twenty-five, years ago.

However, over recent years the pitfalls of inappropriate heating have become better understood, which should affect the decisions taken.

Historic churches are an important part of the nation's past. All who care for them (and indeed for all church buildings) must hand them on in a healthy state to the next generation. Heating systems affect them both directly through their installation and indirectly via the environment they create.

In the past decade there has been increased concern for the environment and global warming, and the need for a prudent and efficient use of energy. Rapid strides have been made in boiler efficiency, electronic controls and design methods, allowing modern systems to be more economical than their predecessors.

Comments, case studies and monitored results are invited by the Council for the Care of Churches in order to assist with future revisions of this publication.

BACKGROUND

A well-heated church is by-and-large a Victorian invention and a late twentieth century expectation. Prior to the re-invention of central heating (given that some Romans had it in the first place), churches were largely unheated, although the privileged few enjoyed a fire or stove which gave local radiant heat.

Today, with widespread domestic central heating and warm cars, many people prepare themselves less well for the cold and expect buildings to be warmer. The need for comfort has hit many churches particularly badly owing to their large volumes, massive and poorly insulated construction, and relatively low intensity of use.

Coal-fired boilers and stoves were difficult to light and slow to warm up, and often were left alight at low level throughout the winter and stoked more vigorously when required. These days, heating is more controllable and is often switched off totally, letting buildings cool down between occupancy times. However, to warm up a traditionally constructed church properly can easily take at least a day; the warming-up process is expensive and often uncomfortable owing to the air currents created in the process, and the intermittent drying and wetting effects can be bad for the fabric.

By modern standards, many church heating systems are inefficient and badly-controlled, particularly for the way the buildings are now used. These are not new problems:

> The usual form of church . . . has four ceilings of three different heights making it difficult to extract the air at the level of the roof. The clerestory windows chill the warm air as it rises, and send it down in a cold douche on the heads of the congregation.

> An architect is instructed to prepare plans . . . Occasionally some too active member ventures to ask the architect if he has made any arrangements for ventilation. He always receives the reply that the subject has received the most careful attention and that when the building is finished it will be found perfect in that respect . . . Eventually the congregation is split between those who prefer rheumatism and bronchitis with open windows or those who prefer asphyxia with the windows shut.

> If economy is the principal object, a cheap hot air apparatus is ordered . . . If wiser councils prevail, hot water pipes are fixed, but as they are generally placed beneath the floor in channels . . . they become speedily covered by a coating of non-conducting dust, and there is generally an unpleasant smell . . . The building is too frequently used but once a week, and is

therefore hastily warmed at the end of the week, an operation very imperfectly performed.

E.H. Jacob, *Notes on the Ventilation and Warming of Houses, Churches, Schools and Other Buildings,* SPCK, 1894

Church heating must not be considered in isolation: the whole system of heating, ventilation, building, contents, users and operations must be taken into account. There are no universal answers: for instance a system which performs satisfactorily in a building with a slate roof might threaten the integrity of a lead roof in an otherwise similar building, owing to different responses to moisture movement.

Changes to heating systems and their operation, or insulation to reduce heat loss, are often made without proper consideration of their effect on the building and the things it contains. In the past, continuous heating often dried things out excessively. The effect on organs was notorious. Today, it is well-known that inappropriate use of heating in housing may cause condensation and deterioration of the building. Similar things also happen in churches and ill-considered alterations could lead to large repair bills years or even decades later.

More efficient heating arrangements, more effectively designed and operated to keep people adequately comfortable at the required times, can cut running costs to a minimum. However, as a result, the church often has less heat put into it than before, though on a more measured basis. Unless the correct steps are taken, it will usually be damper.

1

Human comfort

It is often thought that if a certain air temperature is achieved, people will be comfortable. This is too simplistic; the feeling of comfort depends on the individual's thermal balance - metabolic rate, clothing, and heat loss to the surroundings. This in turn depends not only on the air temperature but on the temperature of the surrounding surfaces and the velocity of any air movement. If the walls are colder, then a higher air temperature is required for comfort. Likewise, people notice air movement (draughts) more at lower air temperatures.

In a small room, air temperature is often a good enough indicator of thermal comfort. However, surface temperatures, air movement and radiation are almost equally important, particularly in large and intermittently heated spaces such as churches and halls. We all experience the effect of a cold floor, of draughts, and of feeling warm in the sun on a cold day, but we often neglect these effects in the design and operation of heating systems. The result is that we often do the wrong things by not getting to the root of the problem. For instance:

- in an attempt to make a building comfortable for an hour or two we also try to heat the whole structure

- the air gets warm at high level rather than where the people are

- in an attempt to warm up the building rapidly we may create draughts which can nullify most of the benefit of the warmth.

To stop heat escaping may not be the only problem. Sometimes:

- windows are sealed but the draughts remain, as they are due to heating-induced downdraughts

- an intermittently-used building is insulated but there is little improvement in comfort or fuel economy, as the problem is more one of system design and the building's thermal capacity than of heat loss to the outside.

Relative humidity is another determinant of human comfort, although at 'ordinary' temperatures a wide range of humidity values will be considered comfortable.

Noise is not often considered in relation to heating, but noise from fans, gas flames, air movement, or from thermostats and relays switching on or off can reduce audibility and lead to irritation and discomfort. Changes in noise level are often more disturbing than a constant low level.

1.1   Thermal comfort

People do not in themselves need heating. The body produces heat by chemically burning up food. The rate depends on physical activity: about 70 watts when asleep, about 100 watts (equivalent to a light bulb) when sitting and listening, perhaps 150 watts when singing vigorously, and much more during heavy manual work. An individual is comfortable when the balance between this and the heat loss to the surroundings is reasonable.

The mechanisms of heat transfer between people and their surroundings are the normal ones of convection, conduction, radiation and evaporation (figure 1.1). In a church the following characteristics are usually found.

Convection is normally the most important. It is a loss from the body, since air even in warm buildings is cooler than the skin. The rate of heat loss is greater if the air is moving, owing to increased convection and evaporation. Losses from exposed parts of the body (generally hands, face, neck and ankles) are particularly important. The sensitivity varies: a refreshing breeze on the face can become an icy draught if it falls on the back of the neck. Cold draughts near the floor and fashions in clothing can cause discomfort in conditions which might otherwise be satisfactory.

Heat transfer by **conduction** is generally quite small, and normally a loss: contact with warm surfaces becomes uncomfortable after a while. However, feet often get cold in a church, owing to a cold floor and draughts at ankle level, and this has a disproportionate influence on perceived comfort. Carpets and cushions give limited, but useful, insulation, and pew or underfloor heating can counteract the effect. When traditional pews are taken out, complaints about heating often ensue because the wooden insulating floor and the barriers to air currents have gone.

The effect of **radiation** on comfort is often overlooked. In normal clothing, radiation and convection are equally important, the radiant proportion falling a little as clothing becomes heavier. The heat exchange process is outlined in figure 1.2. The radiation from any surface is proportional to its area and increases very rapidly with its temperature. Small, high temperature radiant heaters are intense and clearly identifiable. Low temperature sources, such as the internal surfaces

6

Fig 1.1   Heat transfer affecting thermal comfort

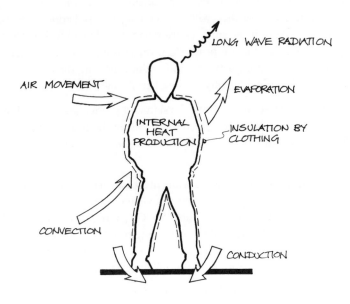

Fig. 1.2   Radiative heat transfer

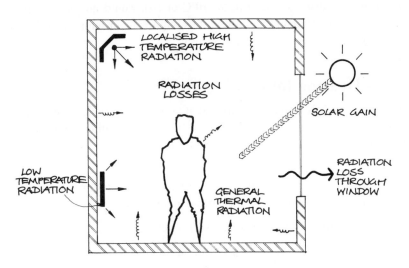

of a building, are also important owing to their large surface areas. People surrounded by cold surfaces (at whatever distance) will feel cooler than if these are at the air temperature, as they will be receiving less radiation from their surroundings. Conversely, if the surfaces are warm, people will feel comfortable at a lower air temperature. Radiant heaters can thus improve comfort when the air is cold, as the sun does on a frosty day, and without heating the building or the air too much, or without incidentally causing bad draughts.

Evaporative heat losses occur from the skin and particularly through breathing and singing, but their influence on comfort during the heating season is usually negligible. The moisture balance is, however, crucial for the building and its contents: see chapter 2.

The variety of heat exchange mechanisms makes air temperature a poor index of thermal comfort unless there is little air movement, and air and surface temperatures are uniform and similar. The UK Chartered Institution of Building Services Engineers (CIBSE) makes its recommendations in terms of 'dry resultant temperature', which in still air is the average of the air and radiant temperatures. Other factors affecting comfort are summarised in figure 1.3.

The CIBSE recommended design value for dry resultant temperature in churches is 18°C (65°F), but for people in outdoor clothing and stockings 15°C (59°F) is perhaps more realistic. Figure 1.4 shows how this may be obtained with a range of radiant and air temperatures. During cold weather, the temperatures of internal surfaces will be low, particularly if the church is heated intermittently, and a mean radiant temperature of 10°C or less would not be uncommon. A resultant temperature of 15°C would thus require an air temperature of 20°C or more, or alternatively some radiant heating.

1.2   Heating for comfort

Where a church is in regular daily use, it may be reasonable enough to achieve comfort by heating the building generally and avoiding stratification and draughts. In a building used less frequently, this may be too expensive. It is wiser to aim to achieve comfort more directly, and first by:

- encouraging the congregation to wear warm clothing, with particular emphasis on protecting their necks and ankles

- providing insulating floor and seat coverings

- avoiding draughts, particularly round the feet.

Fig. 1.3   **Possible sources of thermal discomfort**

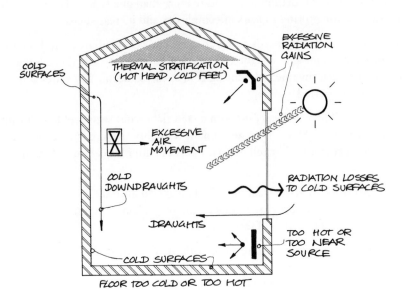

Fig. 1.4   **Result of different radiant and air temperatures**

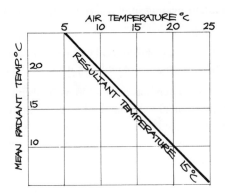

In an intermittently-heated church, a suitable environment in terms of convection, conduction and radiation may require more than one type of heating. This can appear daunting owing to fears of complexity and increased costs.

Heating for comfort only needs to be effective for occupied areas, and for the period of occupation. For instance, heaters to counteract cold downdraughts from windows need operate only during cold spells, at occupancy times and for a short warm-up period.

An unheated building will start off with a cold floor, cold seats and low radiant and air temperatures. However, it need not be draughty as there will be few thermal convection currents. The following options can improve comfort at relatively low cost.

Pew or local floor heating (section 5.7). This is seldom 100% effective but can provide a worthwhile improvement in local air and radiant temperatures and can also reduce the problem of cold feet.

Carefully designed **warm air heating** with good control of air distribution: 'washing' surfaces with a warm air stream can help increase surface temperatures (and hence radiant conditions) without warming the building right through.

Radiant heating is good in theory as it can be localised to the areas where the people are and it also heats the floor and the seats. However, air temperatures should not be allowed to get too low (10°C is a reasonable minimum) and systems must be carefully selected and designed to be effective. It is often difficult in practice to introduce radiant heating unobtrusively and cost-effectively.

In principle a good combination is low level background heating to stop the building and the air becoming excessively cold and damp plus local radiant heating; this can also have advantages for the building itself: see chapter 3.

Sizing an occasional heating system has little to do with design heat loss and pre-heat times: it depends more on the precise building and system characteristics and the comfort requirements. Independent professional advice should always be sought; it is dangerous to assume that an installation that works well in one church will do so in another.

2

Heating, moisture and air movement

Heating systems should be designed to achieve two objectives effectively and economically: to make people comfortable and to help look after the building and its contents. The very act of heating also changes the moisture balance.

Many people assume that heating automatically dries buildings. However, this is only so with regular heating and copious ventilation, as often happened in the past. These days, heating tends to be less sustained, fewer heating appliances draw combustion air from within the church, there is less emphasis on ventilation for health (though this is now re-emerging as an issue), and buildings are instead sealed up to avoid draughts and heat loss. This makes dampness a problem which heating alone may not alleviate.

This chapter discusses the relationship between heating and relative humidity, the generation and control of moisture, and how suitable conditions may be met through planning, system design and operation, and the avoidance of draughts. Chapter 3 then looks at the effects of heating on the fabric and contents of the building.

2.1   Absorption and loss of heat by the building

The easiest way to achieve a comfortable environment is to heat the building thoroughly and to control the air temperatures using a detector at low level, where the people are. All internal surfaces are then warmed up, making radiant conditions reasonably satisfactory.

The rate of heat loss through a building element is termed its U-value, measured in watts per square metre per degree Celsius temperature difference between inside and outside (expressed as W/m^2K). The smaller the U-value, the better the insulation. In traditionally-constructed churches, the heat losses will often be in the following order of decreasing importance: walls (for tall buildings) or roof (if uninsulated, for wide buildings), windows, air infiltration, floors.

11

For new buildings, 1995 Building Regulations AD Part L require the following maximum U-values:

	U-value (W/m²K)
Outside walls, floors and roofs	0.45
Walls to unheated spaces	0.6
Windows, doors and rooflights	3.3

However, existing buildings are often much less well insulated, typically:

	U-value (W/m²K)
335mm (13.5 inch) solid brick wall, with dense plaster	1.7
235mm (11 inch) brick cavity wall, with dense plaster	1.5
Thick stone wall, with lime plaster, about	0.8
Uninsulated roof, about	2.0
Roof incorporating 25mm (1 inch) insulation, about	1.0
Roof incorporating 50mm (2 inch) insulation, about	0.6
Single glazed windows, about	5.5
Stone floor, 30 x 10 metres, uninsulated	0.45
Stone floor, 60 x 20 metres, uninsulated	0.25

Typically 'steady state' heat losses in existing buildings often total about 1 watt per cubic metre of church volume per degree Celsius of temperature difference between inside and outside. In small churches, which have more enclosing surface area and air infiltration in relation to their volume, losses may be relatively higher.

The Design Heat Loss is the rate of heat input necessary to maintain the required internal design temperature under specified external conditions (in the UK often -1°C, with no sun and wind conditions average for the site). Calculation procedures are dealt with in standard works, such as the CIBSE Guide (see further reading).

With intermittent heating, additional heat is necessary to warm up the structure and contents of the building and to counteract their 'cold' radiant effect. A heat pulse travels through a masonry wall at 10-20 mm per hour, so that it can take a day or more to heat even a moderately thick wall. This necessitates a larger heating system than for a more regularly heated building. The thermal capacity has more effect than the insulation on warm-up characteristics, since insulation does not become fully effective until a steady state is achieved. Improving the insulation of massive elements in intermittently and occasionally heated churches may not give the running cost savings which might be predicted, but the result can depend on where the insulation is applied.

For regular daily heating periods, the rate at which heat passes into a structural element (or passes out as it cools down) is termed its 'admittance', also measured in W/m²K. The magnitude of the admittance is governed primarily by the thermal mass and insulation in the first 150 mm (6 inches) of the structure. Typical values are:

	Admittance (W/m²K)
Brick or stone, unplastered	4.5
Brick or stone, with lime plaster	3.5
Brick or stone, with air gap and plasterboard inner lining	2.5
Brick or stone, with insulated plasterboard inner lining	1.0
Uninsulated plaster ceiling	2.5
Plaster ceiling with 25mm (1 inch) insulation	1.2
Plaster ceiling with high insulation	0.8
Stone floor, uninsulated	5.5
Windows, lightweight sheeting etc.	Similar to the element's U-value

For well-insulated heavyweight elements, such as floors and massive walls, the ratio of admittance to conductance can be very large (5 to 10, or more). It is this same sluggish response which accounts for the cool summertime temperatures inside mediaeval cathedrals.

To heat a large church fully is expensive since a large volume of air and massive building elements need to be warmed. Where systems designed for continuous heating are operated intermittently or occasionally, comfort is often relatively poor and energy consumption relatively high because:

● a greater proportion of the heat is used to warm up the system and the building

● with natural convective heating in particular, warming at high level often occurs long before there is much effect lower down

● if the system has been sized for continuous operation, warm-up may take a very long time

● during the warm-up period in particular, draughts are often created which can offset much of the benefit of the warmer air.

13

2.2   The origin and control of draughts

Air movement at room temperature is noticeable if it exceeds about 0.15 metres per second (30 feet per minute), and can be unpleasant at twice this speed. Colder air is perceptible at lower speeds. Figure 2.1 shows the increase in air temperature required to counteract the cooling effect of air velocity. Where there are troublesome draughts, it is usually more cost-effective to tackle them directly, instead of increasing heating generally. Figure 2.2 shows some of the common origins of draughts and figure 2.3 some ways in which these may be controlled.

Fig. 2.1   **Effect of air velocity on resultant temperature**

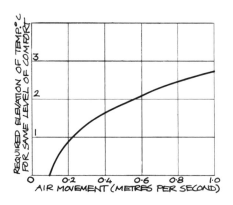

Draughts are frequently a problem in churches. People often think that they are entirely caused by outside air infiltration at doors, windows, eaves, etc. under wind pressures. However other mechanisms, driven by the heating itself, are often more important. These include:

- natural buoyancy of the heated air in the building, leading to outside air ingress at low level via doors, windows, floorboards, grilles, etc., and warm air leaving at high level (e.g. via the tower, roof voids and access doors, and clerestory windows)

- heating-induced natural convection currents, in particular cold make-up air currents, usually at ankle level, necessary to replenish the warm air rising from a heater

- downdraughts from cold surfaces such as tall windows and, with intermittent heating, almost any tall masonry surface

14

- with forced air systems, draughts from the high velocity air if it is too cool, or if grilles are poorly located or adjusted, by induced circulation of room air and along the return air path to the heater.

Draughts are difficult to identify by 'feel'. However, if their causes are not properly understood, one can easily waste money on inappropriate counter-measures. Smoke tests are recommended using a small hand-held 'puffer' or even a cigarette.

It is instructive to observe the velocity and circulation of air currents, particularly near tall windows and convector heaters. Air can 'stick' to a surface in a film very different in temperature to the adjacent air. A downdraught current may thus detach itself from a window sill, continue over the wall surface below, and travel across the floor. These air currents can sometimes be dispersed by introducing turbulence, which can improve local comfort substantially.

Unpleasant downdraughts from glass surfaces and the associated 'cold' radiant effects may also be counteracted by carefully-designed forced warm air systems or by a convector heater at their foot. With tall windows, it may not be possible entirely to neutralise the downdraught, but the cold air may be tempered or deflected out of harm's way (figure 2.3). Double glazing also reduces downdraughts and radiation loss, but is no panacea, particularly for tall windows. Air

Fig. 2.2   Common origins of draughts

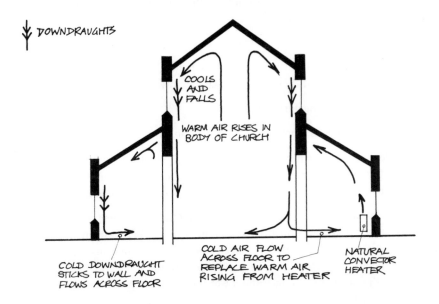

15

Fig. 2.3   Controlling downdraughts from windows

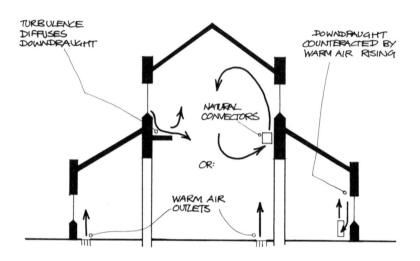

TURBULENCE
DIFFUSES
DOWNDRAUGHT

DOWNDRAUGHT
COUNTERACTED BY
WARM AIR RISING

NATURAL
CONVECTORS

OR:

WARM AIR
OUTLETS

infiltration can attach itself to downdraughts, making them colder still. In a large church with a triforium, cold air from the vault and clerestory may also fall onto the necks of the congregation.

Heat to counteract downdraughts may be introduced by:

- pipes or compact natural convectors beneath the windows (connecting pipework can be difficult to route satisfactorily)

- electric tubular heaters fixed to the sills

- fan convectors or warm air outlets at floor level, as a last resort.

For smaller clerestory windows, deflectors at sill level may help mix the cool downdraughts with warmer air rising from the body of the church. The usefulness and the optimal design of the deflectors are best determined by experiment.

Heating-related draughts may be reduced by effective system operation. For instance, an obvious reaction to cold draughts in the better-warmed part of a church would be to turn up the heat locally. However, this may just accelerate the troublesome air circulation from the colder part to the warmer. It may be better to operate the heating for longer at a lower output, or to provide supplementary radiant heat where required.

Draughts from doors can be of local or psychological significance. A draught lobby is usually desirable, but it needs to be large (otherwise both doors are opened simultaneously) and of good quality; this often makes it too expensive. Instead, good closers and draught seals may be fitted (not inhibiting the operation of the door), perhaps with a curtain or screen to deflect air currents from any exposed seats near the door.

2.3   Stratification

Warm air rises whether it is in church or anywhere else. For slow-acting heating systems it has been shown that there may be little thermal stratification. Stratification is more likely to occur with fast responding, convective and warm air systems, in leaky buildings, and during warm-up.

2.4   Humidity in the air

The balance between heating, ventilation and humidity in buildings is more critical in the British Isles than in most other parts of the world. The warm ocean currents which help to keep the weather mild also fill the air with water vapour, resulting in high atmospheric humidities (particularly in the west) and consistent rainfall in all seasons. Most countries with similar relative humidity are tropical; most with our length of heating season are colder and drier and require heating more continuously.

Atmospheric air always contains moisture in the form of water vapour. The psychrometric curve (figure 2.4) shows how its maximum carrying capacity (saturation humidity) depends on the temperature. For instance, at 4°C air is saturated by about 0.6% of water vapour by weight, while at 14°C it can carry over twice and at 20°C three times that amount. This relationship between temperature and relative humidity is crucial to the influence of heating on the fabric and contents of churches.

Most materials have a volatile moisture content which they exchange with that of the air. The equilibrium content depends principally on the air's 'Relative Humidity' (RH) which is the percentage of the saturation amount at the given temperature. When the air is drier than the equilibrium value, moisture evaporates from the material and, when the RH is above the equilibrium, moisture moves into the material. Figure 2.5 illustrates average daily and seasonal relative humidities of the outside air.

Relative humidities of 70% or more tend to promote condensation, mould growth, and other corrosion and decay processes. Low relative humidities cause organic materials to shrink and become brittle. Since organic materials swell with rising RH and shrink as it falls, fluctuations can cause splitting and make applied materials, such as paints and glues, come away. When the RH fluctuates rapidly, the surface changes its water content and dimensions more rapidly than the underlying material, causing warping and further cracking. Fluctuations can also allow salts in masonry and plasterwork to expand and cause cracking and spalling of surface materials.

A gentle stability is preferable, ideally in the RH range of 45-65%. In practice, 35-75% tends to be acceptable, except where there are specific preservation problems. Sustained RHs above 80% are to be avoided as they lead to moisture contents of 20% or more in timber and other organic materials, putting them at risk of fungal attack.

2.5   Moisture generation

The amount of moisture in the air can increase for a number of reasons, in particular:

- evaporation of water entering as rising damp, rainwater penetration, through structural defects, from pipe leaks and so on

- evaporation from wet clothing

- from flowers and foliage within the church

- transfer of moist air from immediately adjacent areas, such as a tank room, kitchen, servery or crowded church hall

- metabolism, each person introducing about 50 grams of water vapour per hour; more when it is warm or they are speaking or singing, or wearing wet clothes

- combustion of fuels in flueless heaters. This major source of water vapour can lead to severe problems, particularly in poorly-ventilated churches. These problems may not become apparent for a number of years.

In addition moisture evaporates from the fabric of the building, either because it is inherently damp, or because a rising temperature in the church causes evaporation. Often this is the prime source of moisture, particularly in intermittently heated churches.

Moisture within the building is also exchanged with the outside ambient air. Moisture may be removed from the church as damp air escapes through the roof, under doors etc. and by diffusion through the fabric itself; it may also be introduced from outside under certain weather conditions. The inter-relationship between moisture and the building is considered further in the next chapter.

2.6   Condensation

When warm air comes into contact with cooler air or a cold surface, its RH rises, reaching 100% at the so-called Dew Point Temperature (figure 2.6). Condensation then starts:

- as a fog of small water droplets (as when we breathe out on a cold day)

- as a surface film (as when we breathe on a mirror)

- interstitially, in the body of a material (as when we breathe through a scarf).

Surface condensation is obvious on harder, impervious surfaces, in particular glass, tiles and gloss paint. This can be relatively harmless, provided it drains away safely, and mould does not grow. However, stained glass may be affected and suffer damage even when condensation is modest as this allows chemicals to accumulate. Windows can be protected by secondary glazing on the outside with

Fig. 2.4   The psychrometric curve

Fig. 2.5   Typical atmospheric humidities

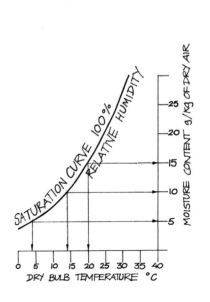

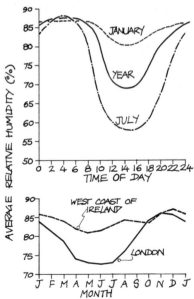

the interspace ventilated to the outside air. Window condensation can be a good warning of the need to ventilate, but it also helps to remove some excess moisture; with double glazing moisture may instead accumulate elsewhere.

Water vapour will often diffuse readily through porous building materials and disperse harmlessly to the atmosphere. However, in a heated building, the temperature decreases towards the outside, and can drop below the dew point, particularly where the porosity of the outer layers to water vapour is less than the inner ones (figure 2.7). Interstitial condensation may then occur, and this in turn reduces the insulating qualities of the materials, leading to increased heat loss and further condensation. Unfortunately, moisture may accumulate in this manner over a long period before it or its effects are noticed.

Interstitial condensation most frequently occurs where insulation is used incorrectly. The source of the moisture may be condensation from the atmosphere or may come from the solid material (e.g. 'rising damp'). For instance, fibrous insulation applied internally may have little resistance to water vapour, but may lower the temperature of the wall behind to less than the dew point, allowing moisture to accumulate. A similar effect may occur where foam-backed carpet is laid over solid floors; this has caused brasses to corrode. Insulation above a ceiling may have little effect on water vapour transmission but, at the lower mean temperature in the roof space, the air change rate is no longer sufficient to remove the excess water vapour or moist air emerging from the building beneath. The air change rate may also have been reduced, deliberately or inadvertently, by blocking openings at eaves etc. when the insulation was applied.

For more detailed information on insulation, ventilation and condensation risks, see *Thermal Insulation: avoiding Risks*, Building Research Establishment, HMSO, 1994.

Fig. 2.6   The condensation process

Fig. 2.7   Interstitial condensation

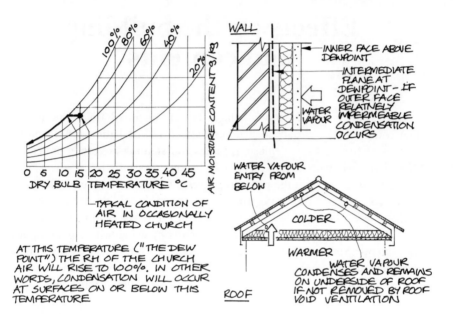

AT THIS TEMPERATURE ("THE DEW POINT") THE RH OF THE CHURCH AIR WILL RISE TO 100%. IN OTHER WORDS, CONDENSATION WILL OCCUR AT SURFACES ON OR BELOW THIS TEMPERATURE

Fig. 2.6 labels:
100% 80% 60% 40% 20%
AIR MOISTURE CONTENT g/kg
0 5 10 15 20 25 30 35 40 45
DRY BULB TEMPERATURE °C
TYPICAL CONDITION OF AIR IN OCCASIONALLY HEATED CHURCH

Fig. 2.7 labels:
WALL
INNER FACE ABOVE DEWPOINT
INTERMEDIATE PLANE AT DEWPOINT - IF OUTER FACE RELATIVELY IMPERMEABLE CONDENSATION OCCURS
WATER VAPOUR
WATER VAPOUR ENTRY FROM BELOW
COLDER
WARMER
WATER VAPOUR CONDENSES AND REMAINS ON UNDERSIDE OF ROOF IF NOT REMOVED BY ROOF VOID VENTILATION
ROOF

3

Effects on the building and contents

Heating systems and the way in which they are operated affect buildings and their contents. The visual and structural effects of installation and the possible dangers of fire, leakage, explosion, fumes and staining are easily understood. Less obvious but often far-reaching in its repercussions is the effect on the humidity of the air and the prevailing levels of moisture in the building's fabric and its contents. As temperature is to comfort, humidity is to preservation, so that there can easily be conflicts between the needs of the church and its contents and the desire to reduce heating costs by using fast-responding heating systems. Stable and moderate humidity levels are best: excessive dryness can cause organic materials to crack and crumble; dampness leads to rot and corrosion; and fluctuations cause condensation and dimensional changes, and salt-related damage.

Temperatures and humidities need to be monitored particularly where there are items of historic importance, and action taken to keep moisture levels within a satisfactory range. This may require better control of ventilation as well as heating. Dehumidification may occasionally be appropriate in intermittently heated churches prone to dampness, but it will only be effective if they are reasonably airtight.

Heating is normally regarded as good for buildings, but heating systems are also known to cause specific types of deterioration. Indeed, some European authorities have concluded that no heating is best. In the British climate a little heating will normally be preferable, with suitable ventilation or dehumidification to avoid relative humidities becoming too high; this is now known as 'conservation heating'.

Unfortunately, economic methods of heating for comfort often cause rapid variations in temperature and humidity levels. Whether this hurts the building and its contents depends very much on the individual situation.

3.1   Consequential effects of heating on the building

Some of the negative effects of heating are obvious, others less so.

Fire   Many fire risks are readily apparent and are minimised by compliance with regulations and codes of practice. Apart from human error, the most common causes are faulty electrical installations and the alteration of boilers without due regard for the construction and capacity of an existing flue or chimney. Portable heaters of all kinds should be avoided; fixed equipment is always preferable. The placing of hassocks against electric under-pew heaters has been known to cause fires and carefully designed approved devices with double overheat protection should be used. Risks from lightning flashovers must be avoided by the correct installation of pipes, supports and metalwork in relation to lightning conductor systems.

Fumes   In a poorly maintained system combustion products may escape, causing a safety and health hazard which should be corrected immediately. Gas and paraffin heaters designed to discharge their combustion products into the heated space require good ventilation to remove both fumes and the water vapour, which is a major combustion product. Excess water vapour can condense and accelerate decay, which may also be exacerbated by the presence of trace chemicals. This type of heater must not be used where the church is constructed of or contains potentially vulnerable items (see section 5.4).

Staining   Streaks above radiators, convectors, pipe brackets and warm air grilles are well known, as is pattern staining on ceilings. Their avoidance is discussed in section 9.4. Liquid fuel may also cause staining and damage, and should be kept out of the church itself.

Condensation and dampness   In recent years a general trend to less ventilation and more intermittent heating has increased problems of condensation and dampness in churches. The relationship between heating, humidity and the health of the church and its contents is considered in detail later in this chapter.

Drying out   Early central heating systems had a reputation for making buildings dry: dampness would disappear but natural materials, such as timbers and organ components, would shrink and crack. Sometimes, where there were faults such as leaky gutters, new heating systems accelerated timber decay and insect attack by making temperatures and humidities more sympathetic to the biological processes. This may also occur during drying out, when materials pass through conditions under which they are most prone to attack. Heating should never be used as a substitute for good maintenance and prompt repairs. Underfloor heating may drive moisture up adjacent walls and columns. Accelerated evaporation of rising damp also permits more water to rise into the building, bringing with it dissolved salts from the ground or from building materials which may cause damage and efflorescence. Wall paintings are known to have been destroyed by this mechanism, particularly where temperatures and relative humidities also fluctuate. Water evaporated from damp parts of the building may subsequently condense on cold surfaces or within materials which were previously dry, leading to further difficulties.

Moisture transfer Intermittent heating can cause the pulsed transference of moisture into and out of the building fabric. Such cyclic effects can activate salts within the structure and can also give rise to 'ratchet' effects, whereby in each cycle more moisture can be absorbed in some elements than released. This can cause moisture to accumulate, for example, in roofs.

Roof structures Warm moist air within a church will tend to escape through the roof under natural buoyancy forces. This can lead to condensation, particularly if the roof is metal-clad or the roof-space is insulated. Condensation can corrode the underside of lead roofs under some circumstances, particularly if ventilation is inadequate. Great care needs to be taken when altering heating and ventilating arrangements, and specialist advice may need to be sought.

3.2   Effects on the contents

Valuable works of art, furnishings and records in a church need a suitable environment, preferably at a stable temperature and moderate relative humidity (see below), and protected from chemical contaminants and dust. Specific requirements are a matter for a conservator. Ideal conditions will not normally be practical, but extremes should be avoided. For instance:

- thin artefacts respond rapidly to changes in temperature and relative humidity and may suffer deterioration where heating is intermittent: authorities recommend a rate of temperature change no greater than 1.5°C per hour

- pictures insulate, causing a lower temperature and a higher relative humidity between them and an outside wall: free circulation of air behind the pictures should be arranged, if possible leaving a gap of 150mm (6 inches)

- where there is stratification, items high on the wall may get quite hot and also suffer because the relative humidity of the adjacent hot air will be lower (although, close to the colder wall, the local relative humidity will be higher than in free air)

- heat emitters and air grilles can place nearby items under thermal stress, whether from radiation, warm air, or merely rapid air movement; staining should also be avoided

- at high relative humidities, damage by chemical pollutants from industrial atmospheres and flueless heaters may be accelerated.

Many of the problems may be alleviated if items are appropriately protected, for instance stored in cabinets with a degree of heat and moisture storage capacity, which 'buffer' the item from the changing external environment. The Parochial Records Storage Cupboard is one example.

3.3   Effects on organs

The organ has often been an early victim of unsatisfactory heating. Advice should be sought from a specialist if major changes to the heating system or its operation are contemplated. The most common problems are:

- excessive dryness generally, usually caused by over-generous heating and ventilation. These can cause organic components to shrink, crack and harden, affecting tune, structural integrity and the pliability of leather in bellows, valves, flaps, etc., and in severe cases much damage can be done. Air temperature settings may need to be lowered, particularly in cold weather (below freezing outside) when the drying effect is harshest.

- local drying of all or part of the organ, owing to heat emitters or pipes running too close to (and sometime even in!) the organ, or warm air or radiant heaters aimed at it, with similar results to the previous point. Heat emitters should be relocated, pipes insulated, and radiant elements and warm air flows redirected.

- intermittent heating, with rapid variations in temperature. Because the velocity of sound in air varies with temperature, this affects the organ tune. It is particularly troublesome if the organ is tuned when the church is unheated and played when it is warm (or worse still, warming-up). The situation can be improved by tuning the organ when the church is warm, and by not letting the building get too cold (say below about 8-10°C) between occupancy periods. This is often a good idea for other reasons.

- stratification of warm air in the church, causing the organ pipes at high level to be warmer than those lower down, consequently affecting tune (and perhaps also moisture levels, particularly where the organ is in a gallery). Stratification is also uncomfortable and uneconomical, and should be minimised as discussed later, particularly in section 8.4.

Note that advisers sometimes appear to confuse the direct effects of temperature (e.g. the third and fourth points above) with the indirect effects of drying out (e.g. the first two points) and may recommend organ humidifiers prematurely and unnecessarily. In an appropriately heated church, humidifiers will not normally be required.

3.4   Effects of intermittent heating

Occasionally heated buildings are particularly prone to condensation. Fast-reacting heating systems give an impression of warmth but the fabric remains cold. While the heating operates, water vapour enters the air rapidly by evaporation from damp materials, from the congregation, and from flueless heaters. Figure 3.1 shows the rate at which moisture can be evaporated from the damp fabric of an intermittently heated church. When air heating is used, the moisture-carrying capacity of the warm air may be sufficient to keep the RH at a reasonable level while the heating operates, although some condensation may occur in places, for example on a stone floor. However, when the heating switches off air temperature may fall rapidly, giving a high RH, high dew points and possibly saturation. Rapid swings in temperature and humidity are also likely to cause articles within the church to deteriorate prematurely.

Fig. 3.1   Effects of intermittent heating
(church heated twice a month)

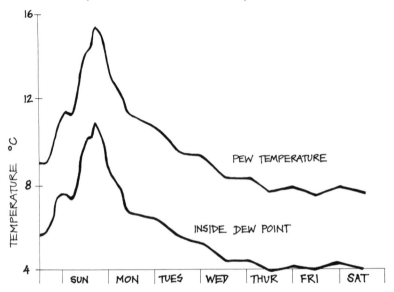

3.5 Roof and ceiling construction

The arrangement of ceilings under church roofs is of four main kinds (figure 3.2).

Direct The underside of the roof forms the ceiling of the church, as with lead roofs over boarding in many village churches. Uninsulated roofs of this kind are potentially at high risk of condensation and care must be taken about any changes to heating and ventilation which might make the church (or the roof) colder, damper, or less well-ventilated. Note that the change to more intermittent heating (even if the church is warmer when the heating is on) or a system which gives less stratification (for example, replacing large column radiators with a more diffuse form of heating) might be sufficient to tip the balance. If the roof is being replaced, consider incorporating insulation, but this needs to be carefully detailed to avoid moisture-related risks.

Fig. 3.2 **Common roof and ceiling types in historic buildings**

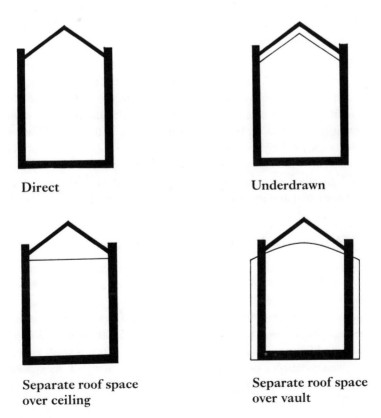

Direct

Underdrawn

Separate roof space
over ceiling

Separate roof space
over vault

Underdrawn There is a separate ceiling, but the space between it and the roof covering is inaccessible and within the structural depth of the roof structure only. In theory this type of roof, particularly if metal-clad, is at a higher risk of condensation than a direct roof, but in practice this is not always so. At present there is a technical debate about the merits or otherwise of ventilating the void space. Take advice.

Separate roof space over a ceiling as in most houses. The roof void space is often inaccessible and may be separately ventilated (directly or adventitiously) by outside air. In theory this works best where the void space is well-ventilated by outside air and in which the ceiling is reasonably impervious to the passage of air and water vapour from within the church. In practice, the ceiling can be quite leaky and, if insulation is added over it or if the church becomes damper, the possibility of moisture-related problems in the roof can increase.

Separate roof space over a stone vault The roof space is often accessible, well-segregated from the atmosphere in the church, and separately ventilated by outside air to some degree. Often void spaces like this are relatively unaffected by changes to the heating, provided that any access doors etc. from the church into the roof space close tightly and are kept shut.

Under certain conditions, condensation can form under the outer roof covering, be it tile, stone, or metal. Slates and particularly metals tend to be most affected owing to their lesser thickness and their imperviousness to moisture. Slates and tiles often have sarking felts or boards beneath, which intercept any condensate and allow it to re-evaporate later and/or to run-out at the eaves. However, with metal roofs - particularly lead, aluminium and zinc - the condensation/evaporation process can lead to corrosion on the underside, particularly where moisture is trapped, and the degree of risk depends amongst other things upon changes to heating, ventilation and insulation. Advice may be necessary.

3.6   Humidity levels inside churches

The first influence on the relative humidity in a church is the moisture content of the outside air which finds its way in. This can be dominant if the church is well ventilated, and significant even if it is apparently sealed. With all windows shut and doors in normal use, infiltration rates are conventionally estimated at 0.25 air changes per hour for a large church (over 7000m^3) and 0.5 in a smaller one, but actual figures can vary substantially. For instance, a small church could well have one air change per hour or more, while in King's College Chapel the measured rate was 1.5 per day.

In the UK heating season, atmospheric relative humidities are commonly above 80% (figure 2.5); 100% is not unusual, particularly with westerly winds and at night. The moisture content (absolute humidity) and dew point of the air remain constant unless water vapour enters or leaves it by some mechanism, so if there are no gains or losses of moisture within the building, the resulting RH in the church may be determined from the psychrometric chart (see figure 2.4).

For instance, if outside air at 4°C and 100% RH enters a building and is heated to an internal temperature of say 14°C, its RH will fall to 50%. Conversely, in springtime the heating might be off and the building structure at the mean outside temperature, again say 14°C. If a warm front were to arrive at 20° C and 80% RH and this air filled the building, condensation would occur. Massive buildings near the west and south coasts are particularly prone to this 'warm weather condensation' and where this occurs one should consider dehumidification or heating when there is a rapid rise in external air temperature.

In an occasionally heated church, provided there is no internal water vapour input, the expected relative humidity often averages about 75-80%. This is just below the danger limit but well above the optimum level. Unfortunately, there are numerous ways in which the moisture level may be increased, as described in section 2.5.

On the face of it, and if the fuel can be afforded, excessive relative humidities can be dealt with by heating. The psychrometric chart shows that for a given moisture content, the higher the temperature, the lower is the RH. However, if moisture is being generated in a church faster than it can get out, it will build up. The excess is normally removed by ventilation, particularly during and following the main periods of use, but this of course also removes heat. A small amount of water vapour will also escape by diffusion.

In practice certain materials, particularly wood, plaster and stone, stabilise the RH by absorbing water vapour from humid air and re-emitting it later. However, the rate of absorption may be slow in relation to the peak output from congregations, tourists, and particularly flueless heaters, the total absorptive capacity may often be limited, and materials may suffer where RHs are consistently too high, too low, or fluctuate too much.

The occasionally-heated church may thus be on the verge of being dangerously damp and ventilation is necessary. Otherwise some small change, such as draughtproofing, leaks not attended to, or the introduction of flueless heaters, may be the last straw. The traditional practice of 'airing' the building on relatively warm (but not humid) afternoons was very helpful.

The alternative can be dehumidification, often using a device which operates in a similar manner to a domestic refrigerator with the door left open, and uses many of the same components. The excess water vapour removed by condensation on a cooled coil runs off into a container or preferably to a drain, while the heat extracted is returned to the building through a second coil. Individual units cost relatively little to run in comparison with heating and ventilation to obtain the same rate of moisture removal, but many units are needed to cope with a large church. For regular use they are most effective where ventilation rates are low. Impressive bucketfuls of water do not necessarily represent a significant improvement in conditions.

In a more regularly heated church, the mean temperature will be higher and mean relative humidities are correspondingly likely to be lower. Indeed, in the past with continuous heating and stoves which caused large amounts of air to move through the church, excessively low RHs were sometimes the problem. This occasionally occurs in warm and well-ventilated buildings today.

3.7   Arranging for ventilation and humidity control

The specific balance between heating, ventilation and usage can cause such variations in relative humidity levels that it is best not to hypothesise. Quick checks can be made using a hygrometer and a maximum and minimum thermometer; these could usefully be left in the church and inspected regularly. Portable instruments such as thermohygrographs and electronic recorders are useful for short-term or longer surveys. In making any measurements it is important to collect both indoor and outdoor data and to use the psychrometric chart to compare them (particularly noting the dew points). Monitoring before and after making major changes to the heating system is highly desirable in any difficult situation: it is becoming more reliable and economic to collect information with modern electronic data-logging equipment. It is recommended that such measurements are always made before and after changing the heating system, preferably during the entire winter. Potential hazards can sometimes be overcome by small alterations to control settings and to ventilation.

It is usually best to have a little permanent background ventilation (unavoidable natural infiltration may be sufficient, particularly in smaller churches without structural dampness, high occupancies or flueless heaters), with means of boosting where necessary. One can use for example:

- wind pressure differences, particularly by cross-ventilation through grilles and windows, which may be fitted with mesh screens to keep out birds and insects

- natural buoyancy (the stack effect). Warm air rises and is expelled through high level openings, drawing in fresh air at lower levels. The ventilation rate increases the warmer the building, and this may lead to excessive heat loss where the air is well heated and stratifies. It is therefore most suitable with radiant and flueless systems

- occasionally, mechanical systems. Fresh air heating and flued heating systems which draw combustion air from the church provide a degree of mechanical ventilation automatically. In principle dedicated mechanical ventilation may be used though in practice it is seldom appropriate or economic. Fans require automatic dampers to prevent unnecessary infiltration and heat loss when they are off. Acoustic treatment will often be necessary if they are to operate while the church is occupied.

Voids above ceilings and roofs, below suspended floors and in cavity walls are designed to be ventilated by outside air to disperse water vapour and avoid condensation. Air bricks, eaves, ridge and other ventilators to these spaces must never be blocked. When ventilation rates to the church proper are reduced and heating and insulation is made more efficient, increased ventilation of voids may become necessary. Impervious tiles, foam carpet backings and underlays over timber floors may also inhibit such 'breathing'.

As a general rule moisture-related problems can be reduced by conservation heating to keep internal surfaces well above the dew point temperature of the outside air, with sufficient ventilation to prevent a build-up of moisture. Many problems could be avoided if windows were left open for a few hours after each service, especially in better sealed and more modern buildings: they now tend to be shut up tight for security and to keep in the valuable heat. Where necessary, it may be convenient to use an extract fan, possibly on a timer which starts, say, 30 minutes after the heating goes off and runs for an hour or two. However, if dehumidifiers are installed, ventilation rates will need to be kept to a minimum.

4

Fuels and heat generation

Fuel choice is often restricted by local availability and by the requirements of the most appropriate and economic heating equipment. Most solid fuel systems have now been replaced or converted to alternative fuels, which have easier control and are less labour intensive, requiring neither stoking nor ash disposal. This chapter therefore concentrates on liquid and gaseous fuels and electricity.

Natural gas, where available, is a common choice as it is usually the simplest of the fossil fuels to use, requiring no storage and needing relatively little equipment maintenance. Over many years its price has been low and relatively stable. Its particular advantages are exploited in a number of special-purpose air, convector and radiant heaters.

Liquefied petroleum gas is considerably more expensive but useful for portable equipment and where natural gas is not available. Fuel oil is most practical in the lighter grades, has been low in cost over recent years, and is a common choice where natural gas is not available.

Electricity is expensive at full rate but, where there is an adequate supply, it can be appropriate for occasional and local heating, owing to high efficiency and potentially good control. Wider use may be possible where off-peak evening and weekend tariffs are available, though with the reorganisation of the electricity industry the future of some of these may be in doubt.

Since all fuel-burning and electrical equipment is potentially dangerous, safe design and use are paramount. While individual proprietary components should be designed to meet safety regulations, the complete installation must also meet building regulations and appropriate codes of practice. Further guidance is available from insurance companies and fire authorities. Insurers should always be consulted before a heating system is installed or alterations are made. Larger heating equipment is usually separately insured and the policy requires regular inspections.

Care must always be taken to ensure that combustible material is not left near to heating appliances. For example, drying teatowels over gas boilers (or indeed, any heating appliance) is dangerous. So is storing chairs or other combustible materials in the boiler room.

4.1   Fuel choice

The following points are important when choosing between fuels.

4.1.1   AVAILABILITY

Gas and electricity may not always be readily available, supply capacity may be limited, and there may be major local variations in the delivered cost of other fuels. The suppliers' initial statements should not be immediately accepted; improved terms can often be negotiated.

4.1.2   MAINTENANCE AND ATTENDANCE

Generally the cost of maintenance increases in the following order: electricity, natural gas, bottled gas, liquid fuel, solid fuel. Attendance costs are lowest for natural gas and electric systems, which are most easily controlled and have no storage and delivery problems. Oil and gas systems require regular servicing (once or twice a year) to maintain efficiency. Solid fuel usually requires daily attendance, even where there is automatic stoking and de-ashing equipment.

4.1.3   INSTALLATION REQUIREMENTS AND COST

As a general rule, equipment and installation costs increase in the order: electricity, gas, light oil, heavy oil, solid fuel. The choice is often, but by no means always, between high capital expenditure to keep running costs to a minimum, or a lower initial outlay and higher operating costs.

4.1.4   FUEL COSTS

The price of fuels is very susceptible to political action, technical changes and market forces. For instance, gas was expensive when it had to be manufactured from coal or oil. North Sea development gave gas a major price advantage. The UK supply of gas is now open to competition. Users of more than 2500 therms per annum (73,200 kWh per annum) can purchase gas from any of the independent suppliers of which there are over fifty. Savings of up to 20% can be achieved but this competitive advantage is likely to be short-lived. The complete gas market is expected to be open to competition by 1998.

Oil prices have tended to fluctuate more, being very high from the mid 1970s to the early 1980s, though from 1985 to 1994 it has often been cheaper than gas.

4.1.5   AIR POLLUTION

Gas tends to be the cleanest-burning fossil fuel. While electricity causes no pollution where it is used, once the overheads of its production are included, its average emissions in the United Kingdom tend to be much higher than for other heating fuels.

Fuel	Carbon Dioxide emission (kg/kWh)
Natural gas	0.21
Fuel oil	0.29
Solid fuel	0.34
Electricity	0.72

Nitrogen oxides (NOx) are also pollutants. Their production depends on the temperature at which combustion occurs and there are now some 'Low-NOx' burners available on the market to reduce the amounts generated.

4.1.6   FUTURE FLEXIBILITY

It is worth considering how systems can adapt to different fuels. For instance, if there was little to choose in capital and running cost between unit heaters and a central system, the central system would normally be preferred, because a change in fuel could be made by altering the heat source only, retaining heat emitters and distribution systems.

Flexibility may also influence the location of equipment. For instance, a gas boiler can be located in many positions, and can use special types of flue. However, if these features are not essential, a wiser choice might be a conventional flue and a location where future supplies of solid or liquid fuel could be arranged.

Systems may also use more than one type of fuel, though the additional complication can be a nuisance. For instance, a low pressure hot water system might use a heat pump as a gentle source of background heat, with a gas or oil-fired unit as a booster. Multi-fuel boilers and stoves are also available, but they are not always as efficient as single-purpose equipment and performance should be checked.

4.1.7   EQUIPMENT CHARACTERISTICS

If a particular form of heating (for example high temperature radiant heating) appears technically the most suitable, it should not be rejected solely because the most appropriate fuel is not the cheapest.

4.2 Fuel oil

Oil is supplied in many different grades. Generally, the more viscous and impure the grade, the cheaper it is, but the more the equipment, its operation and its maintenance cost. Paraffin (Class C1) is used in flueless heaters; kerosene (Class C2, or '28-seconds' oil) is used in domestic boilers; and gas-oil/diesel oil (Class D, or '35-seconds' oil) is used in medium sized boilers and air heaters. Heavier oils are seldom used in churches today.

Prices can vary significantly with supplier and contract details, and competitive quotations should be obtained. It may be possible to join purchasing groups and enjoy bulk rates.

4.2.1 OIL TANKS

Oil tanks can be difficult to locate satisfactorily. Normal practice is to provide storage for at least three weeks' continuous operation. Potential suppliers should be consulted about filling arrangements, particularly if the proposed fill point is more than 18 metres from where the tanker can park.

Tanks need not be adjacent either to the boiler or to the fill point, but a compact layout is preferable, with the fill point beside the storage tank, to reduce the risk of undetected spillage. The fill pipe should fall continuously towards the tank. For remote tanks a reliable alarm, and preferably an interlock, is essential to protect against overflows. Exposed external oil lines should be insulated and ideally protected with heating tape, since Class D oil can freeze in abnormally cold weather. Oil feed lines should preferably be of corrosion-protected steel, since this is not easily damaged.

Above-ground tanks are unsightly but may be camouflaged; provision should be made to inspect and paint all round. There is a small fire risk, so they should be away from lightning conductors and preferably windows. Corrosion-protected steel tanks may be buried, anchored where necessary to avoid displacement by groundwater, and with a manhole for periodic inspection. Reinforced concrete underground tanks with ceramic linings are long lasting but expensive. Plastic tanks are also available but should be sited remotely from the building.

Internal tanks must be placed in fire-resisting chambers, ventilated to the outside air, with a catchpit or bund to retain the entire contents plus a safety margin. Catchpits are sometimes required for external tanks especially where leakage could enter the church or adjoining properties, or pollute watercourses. Plastic tanks must have a catchpit, or double-walled tanks are available. Where oil burners are at high level (e.g. in the tower) leakage could be catastrophic. A small daily service tank should therefore be fitted and filled as required from the main reserve tank.

4.2.2   OIL BURNERS

Heating oils do not ignite unless heated or vaporised by other means. Three main types of oil burner are usually found in churches:

- **wicks** burn quietly but require regular attention and are only found in portable and domestic equipment

- **vaporising burners** are used in small boilers and stoves; the simplest and quietest (found in unit heaters, small domestic boilers and warm air units) use natural draught and heat alone to vaporise the oil

- **pressure jet burners** permit precise control of combustion and are most common in church oil boilers. The fuel, heated if necessary, is forced through an atomiser and mixes with blown air. They are noisy and equipment usually needs to be in its own room. Regular maintenance is essential.

Vaporising burners may be gravity fed while pressure jets require pumps, which are usually part of the boiler. Pumped transfer is generally preferred as a leak is less likely to cause a major flood.

If there is a fire, or if the burner fails to light, oil must be shut off. Integral burner controls allow for most eventualities but a fire valve should also be installed; this is held open by a wire containing fusible links which melt at about 60°C, with a manual quick-release device or equivalent electrical mechanisms. Fire valves are also a useful precaution with high-rated gas-fired equipment.

4.3   Natural gas

Gas is currently relatively low in cost, no storage is required, it can often be burnt quietly in the church itself in a variety of unit heaters, and equipment and flues are relatively simple to install and monitor. Natural gas is not poisonous, but there is an explosion risk. Safety interlocks are incorporated in British Gas Approved appliances to avoid leakage of unburnt gas. If any leakage is suspected, published safety precautions should be followed. Installation is subject to the Gas Act and Gas Safety Regulations and must be carried out by a Registered Installer. Air is needed for combustion of gas (and all fossil fuels) and it is essential that the requisite openings are provided.

Supplies from nearby mains should not be taken for granted: there may be high connection charges or limitations on available capacity. Tariffs can vary and should be discussed with supply companies at an early stage. For larger users, which includes some churches, supplies can be obtained from independent suppliers via British Gas pipelines.

Gas meters should be at ground level in a well-ventilated area, as near as possible to the site boundary. For larger installations, the supply authority may require a separate meter house near the boundary line.

Gas is suitable not only for conventional stoves and boilers but for direct radiant and air heating equipment. Two main types of burner are used:

- **atmospheric burners** are widely used in small convector stoves and radiant heaters and on some larger heaters and boilers; they are usually quiet, although ignition noise can be distracting. Some units have fan-assisted draught, which gives more flexibility in flueing and can improve efficiency by avoiding heat loss to excess combustion air, particularly where a boiler is on low fire or off. Ignition is preferably electrical in order to avoid pilot light fuel wastage.

- **forced draught gas burners** are similar to oil pressure jets, and are normally the more efficient. They are essential in systems where other fuels may be burned, either in a multi-fuel boiler or in order to simplify future conversion.

4.4   Liquefied petroleum gas (LPG)

Liquefied bottled gas is an expensive alternative to natural gas, but useful where there are no mains supplies and for self-contained portable equipment. Leakage is a fire and explosion risk: cylinders should be stored in limited quantities away from combustible materials in a well ventilated place, preferably outside. All equipment, pipe and hose connections should be well maintained and regularly inspected. The widespread use of flueless gas appliances may also cause problems as discussed in chapter 5.

For larger installations, LPG may be delivered by tanker and stored in large spheres or cylinders. Since the gas tends to lie on the ground when released, bulk storage vessels must be away from buildings, fenced in or otherwise isolated from tampering, and open to the air; they can be obtrusive and are best concealed by planting. Prices may vary considerably depending on the amounts required and the use made of the fuel locally.

4.5   Flues

Combustion of all fossil fuels generates gases and moisture which must be dispersed, usually via a flue or chimney, though some heaters have no flue at all (see section 5.4). Except for so-called 'room-sealed' heaters, a supply of combustion air must be provided from the outside. Regulations have been tightened over recent years and must be followed rigorously.

Alternative types of flue are available for gas and some small oil heaters which can make their installation more convenient.

- **conventional flues and chimneys** require appropriate and correctly sized liners according to the fuel being burnt. Regulations regarding the siting and routing of flues and their termination must be followed. Flue gases normally travel up a chimney by buoyancy-driven convection but, where flue gas temperatures are low (for example from a condensing boiler), fan assistance may be necessary. Access points should be provided to the flue, and drainage facilities for any condensate.

- **balanced flues** (figure 4.1) are widely used in domestic gas boilers and room heaters. The burner obtains combustion air and discharges fumes through a wall or roof terminal designed to equalise any wind pressure differences. In favourable circumstances, conventional gas and light oil boilers may also be installed in a sealed compartment with the air intake surrounding the flue terminal. Fan-assisted balanced flue heaters and boilers are also available; their smaller flue size increases flexibility in installation and with good designs the better control of combustion air volume raises overall efficiency, though not always by enough to pay for the electricity for the fan! Balanced flue terminals can have poor external appearance, and fan-assisted versions tend to be smaller and neater. When contemplating the installation of either sort of flue terminal, care needs to be taken over any archaeological implications, the possible damage to external stonework from the products of combustion, appearance, and the possible disturbance of rubble-fill in old walls.

- **dilution flues** (figure 4.2) provide a fan-assisted stream of air in a duct into which the fumes are discharged and diluted to a safe concentration to be blown out through a grille. They are useful where there is no alternative, but the electrical costs of running the fan can be significant.

At low outside temperatures and high relative humidities, water vapour discharged may form a fog around balanced and dilution flue wall terminals, particularly with condensing boilers (see section 6.2). Although normally harmless, visually it can be a nuisance.

Fig. 4.1   Balanced flues

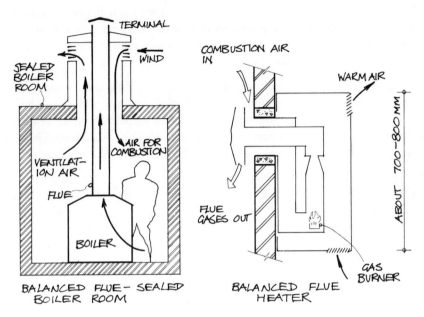

BALANCED FLUE - SEALED BOILER ROOM

BALANCED FLUE HEATER

Fig. 4.2   Dilution flues

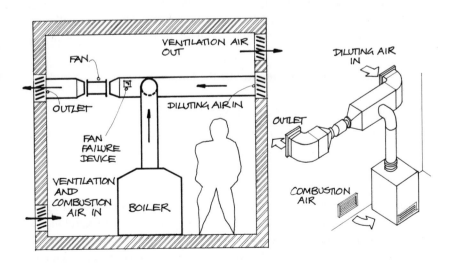

4.6   Electricity

Electric heating often has the lowest installed cost but the high price of standard rate electricity often limits applications to local and occasional heating requirements. It is very useful for bringing heat, particularly radiant heat, to occupants rather than heating the whole building.

Where electricity is used efficiently, off-peak rates can sometimes be comparable with other heating fuels. Since the off-peak period is usually in the small hours, the heat normally has to be stored. However, owing to the high thermal capacity and slow response of many churches, off-peak electricity may sometimes be used directly for background heating and to take the chill off in the early hours.

Tariffs and supply arrangements should be negotiated with the supplier at an early stage before any choice of equipment and operating procedures are agreed. Regional electricity companies normally offer a weekend restricted hours tariff or an evening and weekend 'community tariff' at reduced rates. Caution: outside the weekend or evening periods, charges are often *above* the standard rate.

For the larger consumer, a maximum demand tariff charges for the highest rate of consumption, as well as the total amount of electricity used. This tariff is seldom appropriate for churches, as it is expensive where electric heating is intermittently or occasionally used. Tariffs should be reviewed from time to time; it is not unusual to find that you are paying too much. Suppliers seldom take the initiative in suggesting changes, but usually respond helpfully on request.

As with gas, alternative electricity suppliers now exist for the largest customers, but very few churches currently fall within this category. However, smaller users are also expected to have more freedom to choose their electricity supplier within a few years.

Electricity may be converted into heat by the following means.

4.6.1   DIRECT RESISTANCE HEATING

The current is passed through resistance wires inside a protective enclosure. Examples are electric convectors, air heater batteries and many radiant heaters.

4.6.2   INDIRECT RESISTANCE HEATING

The resistance element heats a material which in turn gives out heat. Examples are floor heating, immersion heaters, oil-filled electric radiators, tubular and lamp heaters. The potentially hazardous electric element is separated from the outside environment and can be fitted with an added safety device, often a high temperature cut-out; this type is generally preferred in churches.

4.6.3   STORAGE HEATING

Resistance elements heat blocks in off-peak periods; the blocks give out their heat then and subsequently. Economic control is difficult, particularly for buildings in occasional use, but fan-assisted versions can be useful where a quick boost is required. Off-peak electricity may also be used in purpose-designed systems using building elements (particularly floors) or tanks of water for heat storage.

4.6.4   HEAT PUMPS

Electricity (or indeed other fuels) may be used in a refrigeration system in reverse to take heat from the outside air, the ground, or a water source (for example, a lake) and transfer it into a building by means of warm air or warm water; this allows more heat to be transferred than its equivalent in fuel consumed. However, on-peak electricity is relatively expensive so the result is seldom competitive with conventional gas- or oil-fired heating. The heat is also at a low temperature (generally 60°C or less) which restricts applications to warm air and low temperature convection and radiant heating. The ratio between the heat output and the energy consumed is known as the coefficient of performance (COP). Heat pumps are worth considering in special circumstances and for new, intensively used, well insulated buildings, but seldom for occasional heating requirements. Controls, reliability and quoted values of COP need to be carefully scrutinised for all intended applications.

4.7   Solar heating

Solar collectors and heat transfer systems are only cost-effective for sustained year-round needs, for example in swimming pools and occasionally for domestic hot water systems. However, by their nature, old churches with massive walls already absorb and store solar radiation over fairly long periods, contributing to their internal heating needs, particularly in spring and autumn. Using the building to trap the sun's heat in this way is known as passive solar heating. On a shorter timescale solar heat can also be exploited in new buildings for example by incorporating south-facing windows, with suitable methods of shading them to avoid glare and overheating, and inbuilt thermal capacity to store the heat. In existing buildings, the roof space can get hot on sunny days and there have been proposals to use a thermostatically-controlled fan to blow this air down into the church. However this is most unlikely to be cost effective and would not eliminate the need for a conventional heating system.

5

Heat emitters

Heat emitters are often regarded as a necessary evil, their most desirable properties being cheapness and invisibility. Such criteria, however, may lead to a high running cost. The varying characteristics of different types of heater need to be understood, and so they are discussed at some length. Well-selected and located radiant and forced warm air heaters may potentially give the best comfort with the lowest running costs, but in practice they can be difficult to incorporate. Natural convectors are more common: these require care in design to avoid draughts and heating the vault instead of the congregation. Portable heaters can be a fire risk, and gas- and oil-heaters without flues require careful attention to ventilation rates, humidity levels, and conservation of valuable parts of the building's structure and contents. Heaters with a large radiant component in their output can usefully improve comfort conditions in small parts of the church (e.g. for a baptism or a choir practice); other local heating may prove disappointing, unless in fully enclosed rooms.

Heat emitters are initially classified according to whether their heat output is primarily as radiation or to the air. Other relevant classifications are then considered, particularly flueless and local heating. Central heating and controls are dealt with in chapters 6 and 7.

Unfortunately, certain heaters, otherwise technically satisfactory, look ugly. This is more a problem of product design than of technical requirements. Users should encourage manufacturers to make improvements; some will depart from their standard ranges if pressed, or may be interested in developing new products. More collective action by groups of potential customers will help to accelerate this development.

In specifying heat emitters, the safety of users needs to be considered. Many radiant heaters can burn individuals or ignite material which is too close to them. Even panel radiators can cause burns, especially to the young and the old. Low surface temperature (LST) equipment is available from most manufacturers. Direct electric heaters will overheat if accidentally insulated (e.g. by hassocks, furniture, or a pile of clothing) and can be a serious fire hazard unless appropriate cut-outs are fitted.

5.1 Radiant heaters

All radiant heaters produce electromagnetic radiation, largely in the infra-red, which is identical to light in all but wavelength. This radiation is emitted spontaneously from any heated object, the total quantity increasing rapidly and the average wavelength reducing as it becomes hotter.

Radiant heaters may be placed in four groups according to wavelength: short wave (white heat), medium wave (red heat), long wave (black heat) and low temperature (normal hot water temperatures). The first three types have very hot elements and produce intense radiation which may ignite materials placed too close to them; they must therefore be installed and positioned with great care. The shorter the wavelength, the more compact the source (size ratios for the four classifications being typically 1:20:300:4000) and the greater the proportion of radiation to total heat output. Short wave sources, being small, can potentially be focused very well; medium wave sources quite well, long wave somewhat, and low temperature hardly at all. Reflectors, where fitted, should be kept clean.

Air is relatively transparent to short wave radiation but components, particularly water vapour, absorb some longer wavelengths more strongly. The absorption increases with moisture content and adds to the inevitable fall-off in radiant intensity with distance, making it important to keep radiant heaters fairly close to the people, even though aesthetically this may be difficult.

Atmospheric absorption is less important for short wave heaters. With short-wave radiation people may also feel comfortable under greater intensities and greater asymmetry than with other heaters, partly because the short wave radiation penetrates clothing and the skin more deeply and so is absorbed more uniformly.

Radiant heaters have an immediate effect on thermal comfort without first having to warm the building or the air. Fast-responding units are thus well-suited to occasional heating needs and to improving comfort in small parts of an otherwise unheated, or poorly heated building. However, the building may still feel uncomfortable if the air and surfaces are too cold (see chapter 1) or if the radiant intensity is too great. Valuable objects should not be exposed to too much radiation as they may be damaged, both through direct heating and by the associated drying effect. The plumes of hot air which rise from the heaters may also damage sensitive objects.

5.1.1 SHORT WAVE RADIANT HEATERS (see figure 5.1)

Short wave heaters are necessarily electric, relying either on electronic processes or on high temperatures not attainable by normal burners. The most common types are lamps designed to maximise the infra-red radiation. Any temptation to use these heaters as the sole source of light should be resisted, and where the light is a nuisance, filters may be fitted which leave only a red or yellow glow.

The lamps most commonly used are:

- mushroom-shaped with integral reflectors, like spotlight bulbs, and with relatively low outputs: they can be useful for local needs, for example to make things a bit more comfortable in the pulpit or for the organist

- tubular with external reflectors, commonly referred to as 'Quartz' radiant heaters: these have higher outputs (typically 750 to 3000 watts each), and units with multiple lamps can heat several hundred square feet (tens of square metres) at a time.

The lamps reach their full output very soon after switching on, making them very useful for intermittent comfort heating requirements, provided their appearance is acceptable and electrical supplies have the necessary capacity. As with most radiant heaters, they should be switched on a little before occupation in order to help warm up the floor and seats. Although good at improving comfort locally, they do not heat the building or the air much generally, so there may be problems of dampness unless there is also either background heating (with suitable ventilation) or dehumidification. The relatively high cost of electricity makes them less economic for more sustained heating needs. The heaters can be installed with little damage to the building structure but can be visually intrusive. Those with a red glow are not always appreciated in a church! Customer satisfaction is variable, both to appearance and to comfort. Early heaters had simple on/off switching, often manually controlled, which could lead to problems of overheating in mild weather or with high occupancy. Some suppliers now provide solid-state proportional control of output.

5.1.2   MEDIUM WAVE RADIANT HEATERS (see figure 5.2)

Medium wave heaters are characterised by their red to yellow glow, like open coal and wood fires. Today, the main fuels are gas and electricity.

The electric versions usually have coiled elements enclosed in silica tubes, with a reflector behind; they are usually attached to walls or suspended from the ceiling. Being relatively low in output, they are most often used for local heating.

The gas-fired units are more powerful, with ceramic radiant elements heated directly by the flame, as in domestic gas fires. They are usually mounted at high level for safety and to get a good spread of radiation. Since reflectors are at best rudimentary, their radiation is less focused than with the electric heaters. Their

Fig. 5.1   **Short wave radiant heaters**

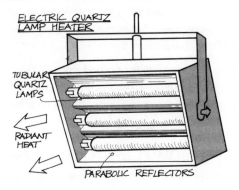

Fig. 5.2   **Medium wave radiant heaters**

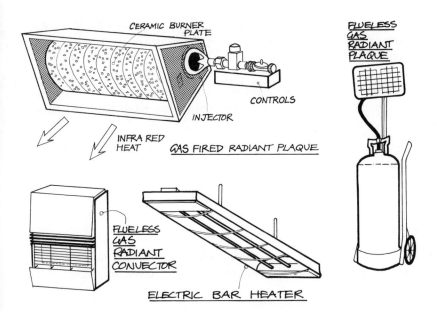

heating effects are partly by direct radiation, partly re-radiation from other surfaces, and partly from direct and indirect heating of the air. There is ignition
noise and a slight hissing from the burners. Most available units are flueless,
which can give problems: see section 5.4.

Portable flueless units are available for bottled gas, ranging from the small floor-
standing domestic heater to industrial units with a large cylinder at the base and
the element at the end of a long neck. They are not recommended; fixed equipment is safer.

5.1.3   LONG WAVE RADIANT HEATERS (see figure 5.3)

Long wave heaters are mounted at high level on walls or suspended from ceilings;
horizontal mounting is preferable as it minimises heat loss by convection. At
about 300°C, their surfaces do not glow but can nevertheless ignite organic materials such as wood or paper. The necessary radiant surface area for a given output
is larger and the heaters often take a linear form, which can sometimes be easier
to accommodate architecturally than individual units.

In the gas-fired units, a fan draws the combustion gases from the burner through
a tube mounted in front of a reflector. Heat from the tube is then radiated and
convected into the church. The units may be either modular, with a straight or
U-tube, or linear, with a long tube having several burners along its length and an
exhaust fan at the end.

The heaters may be either flued or flueless: flueing is easier for the linear system
where fume extract is centralised. A flued system which draws its combustion air
from within the church is usually best as it also provides limited mechanical ventilation. Noise from air intakes, burners, extract fans, and from thermal
expansion and contraction of the tubes and reflectors, needs to be minimised by
careful selection and design. If necessary the fan can be silenced and mounted
outside.

Electric 'black' heaters are available in strip or panel form. Their poorer radiation characteristics and the absence of reflectors makes them generally less
suitable for occasional heating than short and medium wave units, while for more
sustained heating gas heaters would often be more economic. One type of strip
heater has pivoting elements which permit limited control over the direction of
the radiation.

High pressure hot water or steam pipes, with or without reflectors, are also useful long wave radiant sources, but are no longer common owing to safety
requirements.

Fig. 5.3   Long wave radiant heaters

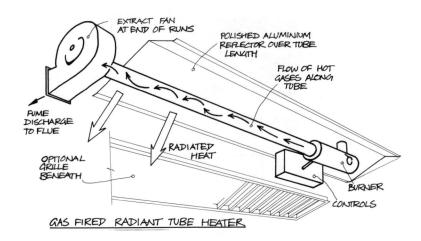

EXTRACT FAN
AT END OF RUNS

POLISHED ALUMINIUM
REFLECTOR OVER TUBE
LENGTH

FLOW OF HOT
GASES ALONG
TUBE

FUME
DISCHARGE
TO FLUE

RADIATED
HEAT

OPTIONAL
GRILLE
BENEATH

BURNER

CONTROLS

GAS FIRED RADIANT TUBE HEATER

U-TUBE GAS FIRED
RADIANT HEATER

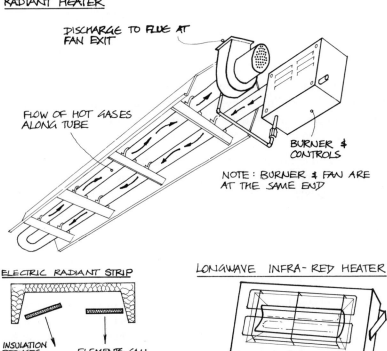

DISCHARGE TO FLUE AT
FAN EXIT

FLOW OF HOT GASES
ALONG TUBE

BURNER &
CONTROLS

NOTE : BURNER & FAN ARE
AT THE SAME END

ELECTRIC RADIANT STRIP

INSULATION
REDUCES
CONVECTION
LOSSES

ELEMENTS CAN
BE ANGLED AS
REQUIRED

LONGWAVE INFRA-RED HEATER

Fig. 5.4   Low temperature radiant heaters

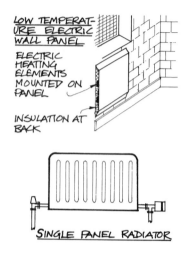

5.1.4   LOW TEMPERATURE RADIANT HEATERS (see figure 5.4)

Low temperature radiant heaters fall into two main groups: panels which operate at normal hot water temperatures (45-80°C); and wall, floor and ceiling heating with surfaces only a few degrees above room temperature. Many only just qualify to be called radiant, as much of their output goes directly into the air and structure of the building. They are most suitable either for localised heating, or where the building and the air are to be warmed generally; the additional radiation makes one comfortable at a rather lower air temperature.

The most common examples are the hot water single panel radiator and various electric heating panels. About half of their heat output is by radiation but, unless the radiator is free-standing, nearly half falls on the wall behind. For hot water radiators heat loss through the wall behind may be reduced by insulation, aluminium foil or pre-formed plastic sheets. However this also reduces overall heat output and panel sizes may sometimes need increasing. Foils should not be used on damp walls otherwise moisture will be trapped. Uninsulated electric panels must never have insulation added on site as they will overheat.

To get full advantage of the radiation, panels should be placed above head level, but this is seldom practical. If mounted nearer the floor, they can overheat the people nearby while hardly being noticed by those further away. They are therefore best used either for whole church heating, positioned at some distance from seats, or close by at low output for very local heating.

5.2   Ceiling, floor and wall heating (see figure 5.5)

Wall, ceiling and floor warming are invisible forms of low temperature radiant heating, with the Roman hypocaust as the historical precedent. Today, hot water or electric heating elements may be embedded in walls, ceilings or floors, or placed behind them. This form of heating causes no staining, and by improving radiant temperatures permits comfortable conditions to be achieved at lower air temperatures. However, it is usually expensive and, since it must warm the structure first, it is most suitable for continuously heated buildings. If buried heating elements are damaged or break down, repair or replacement is often disruptive and expensive.

Ceiling heating is normally provided either by electric heating mats behind plasterboard, or by hot water pipe coils behind a metal ceiling. Very good insulation is required above to avoid excessive heat loss. The air immediately below a heated ceiling is not particularly hot since heat can only move down by conduction, radiation and forced circulation; the main mechanism of heat emission (provided the ceiling is horizontal) is by radiation to the floor. However possible applications in existing churches are very limited.

Floor heating can sometimes be considered for new buildings and major alterations. It can help produce good comfort in continuously heated buildings without stratification, but is less appropriate for intermittent heating for which it can also be relatively expensive to run. The slow rate of response also makes it better for background heating than for full heating. To avoid swollen feet, floor temperatures are limited to about 25°C (77°F) in spaces where people are for several hours, or 28°C (82°F) for intermittent occupancies and in circulation areas. Consequently, the maximum heat output is about 70 watts per square metre, and supplementary heat is usually necessary in tall spaces, most existing buildings and under large windows to counteract downdraughts and the 'cold' radiant effect.

Off-peak electric floor warming, popular in the 1960s, fell from favour largely through inflexibility of control and increases in fuel costs. Improved technology and better-insulated buildings are creating some new interest, though a hot water system will often be preferred owing to the lower fuel cost and in order to widen future fuel choice. Electric heater cables may be embedded or withdrawable; withdrawable is best to simplify repairs. Low-voltage systems using a metal grid embedded in the screed are also available.

Floor warming by hot water is enjoying renewed popularity in well-insulated and regularly heated buildings, owing to advances in pipe materials, underfloor insulation, and new types of concrete screeds. The new systems respond faster and can also make good use of low temperature hot water, which also improves the efficiency of condensing boilers and heat pumps. Small bore pipes are buried in

Fig. 5.5   Ceiling and floor heating

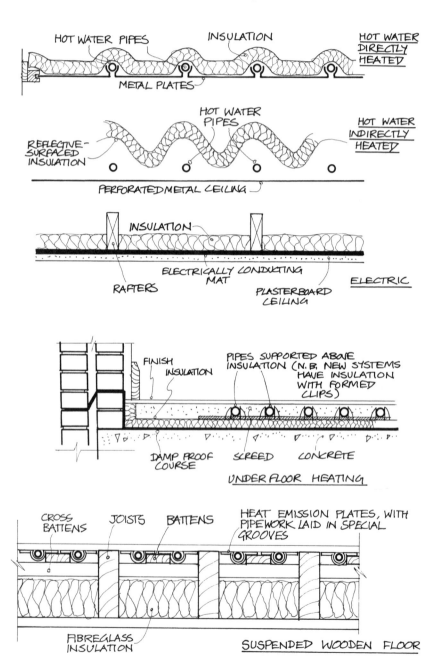

continuous lengths, joints being made in accessible header ducts or preferably in a manifold. Steel tube was used traditionally, owing to its low cost and good resistance to damage during installation. Copper then became more popular, being in long coils and with better corrosion resistance; it was often plastic coated for further protection. Plastic tube alone is now widely used, with installation simplified using proprietary insulation panels complete with pipe supports. Installation and screeding should always be by specialist contractors and with a long-term warranty including the problems of corrosion which may arise if oxygen diffuses through the pipes and into the system. Installation can also be beneath wooden floors in appropriate circumstances, but in all cases the pipes need to be sufficiently far below the surface, or protected by steel plates, to minimise the risk of damage from nails or other fixings throughout the life of the system.

Hot water underfloor systems require careful control of circulating temperatures owing to problems of thermal expansion, overheating, and possible damage to plastics. The floor covering affects the output and the heating affects the floor finish: details may need amending. For instance, stone and marble slabs must be continuously bedded (not placed on dabs), drying-out requirements and adhesives must be suitably specified, and any subsequent changes to floor coverings (in particular adding a carpet) can cause problems. Specification advice should be sought from installation specialists and the heating and flooring manufacturers.

5.3 Convective heaters

Most heaters are predominantly convective, including many so-called radiators. There are two main types: natural convectors which use the buoyancy of warm air to promote heat transfer and forced convectors which use a fan.

5.3.1 NATURAL CONVECTION

The main problem with natural convectors is also the mechanism by which they work: hot air rises. In tall spaces, this frequently makes the temperature high up in the vault greater than that in the nave (figure 5.6). This stratification not only deprives the occupied part of the church of heat but also increases the overall heat loss, owing both to the greater temperature differences and to the additional air infiltration induced. To add insult to injury, the convection currents often cause draughts.

Common types of natural convector are outlined in the following paragraphs. The more extended vertically and the hotter the convecting surface, the more buoyant the air emerging and the greater the resulting air velocities and likely draughts. High temperature and high output units, although attractively

Fig. 5.6   Heating and stratification

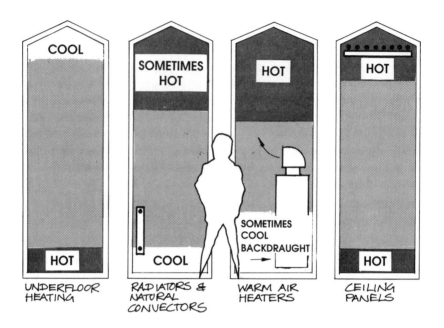

compact, can be disappointing in their results; more gentle, less concentrated sources are preferable for tall spaces.

5.3.2   SOLID FUEL STOVES WITHIN THE CHURCH

Solid fuel stoves used to be widely used in churches, but today they are almost extinct. Occasionally, they have been converted to oil or gas. Their surfaces are often extremely hot and they produce plumes of very hot air which can stratify and also desiccate objects in the rising air stream.

5.3.3   OIL, GAS AND ELECTRIC STOVES

Most modern units are light and compact, with relatively high air discharge temperatures. Where they are operated locally or intermittently in large and tall spaces, they may cause bad draughts and stratification. More massive units tend to produce a gentler heat, with a greater radiant component, but their high thermal capacity and slow response make them less suited to intermittent heating. Where the oil and gas heaters are flueless, the fumes and water vapour may cause problems.

5.3.4   RADIATORS

Radiators range from traditional cast-iron types to the ubiquitous pressed steel. Non-traditional materials are also available, including copper, aluminium and plastic; advantages are claimed but there are also problems. For instance, mixed metals in a system may promote corrosion, and new materials may deteriorate over time and can be more easily damaged. Anti-corrosion additives should normally be used in heating systems with steel radiators, unless absorbed air is effectively removed from the system; high efficiency de-aerators are now becoming available for this purpose. Robust products should be specified: some domestic radiators have only a 10-year design life. Radiators take four main forms (figure 5.7):

- column, with a battery of vertical fins

- single panel, with a flat or corrugated plate

- multiple panel, with several single panels connected to a common header

- radiant convector, normally a flat panel with profiled convective elements added.

Single panel radiators give the best ratio of radiant to convected heat (approximately 1:1) and the lowest tendency to stratification but the required surface area is greater than for other types. Radiant convectors can be very useful at skirting level and for downdraught prevention, and modern patterns can be unobtrusive. Metallic paint should not normally be applied to radiators as it cuts the radiant heat output.

5.3.5   CONVECTORS

Air enters at the base of the unit and emerges at the top or front; front discharge reduces the risk of staining walls, provided the case is well sealed. Low surface temperatures limit the radiant output but are safer and avoid roasting people close by. Convectors give great flexibility to obtain a given heat output and air discharge temperature in a restricted space, but the resulting heat and air distribution is not always good, particularly in tall churches and in the centre of wide churches with perimeter systems. Skirting convectors are useful and unobtrusive, but need careful specification to withstand wear and tear.

5.3.6   PLAIN OR FINNED TUBE

Old installations frequently used plain cast iron pipe. The large volume of water contained makes the systems slow to respond, while the heating surface is often too small for today's requirements. There are however a few systems which are still operated for continuous background heating and can achieve good comfort

Fig. 5.7 Radiators and natural convectors

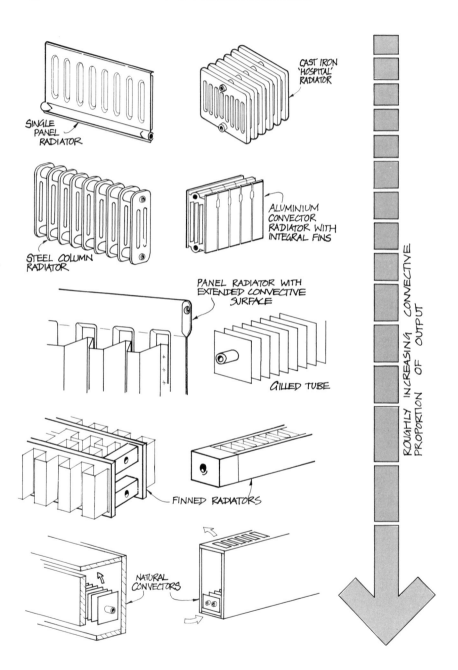

levels and a relatively dry church. Where pipes run under floor grilles, the output is further decreased, especially when ducts are filled with dust and dirt. Pipe coils beneath windows can be effective at reducing downdraughts, but compact convectors are usually preferable. Finned or gilled tube emits more heat than plain but is normally best concealed, though sometimes its industrial appearance can work architecturally. Its heat output drops when dirty, so cleaning should be arranged every few years.

5.3.7 FORCED CONVECTORS AND WARM AIR UNITS (see figure 5.8)

Fans pass air over a heat exchanger, which may be heated directly by electricity or a burner, or indirectly by hot water or steam. In some flueless oil- and gas-fired units (often confusingly called direct air heaters), the air is passed over the flame itself. Gas and oil-fired burners, particularly the larger ones, can be noisy and their performance should be checked carefully and comparable working installations visited before making a selection. Given adequate care in design and installation, acceptable noise levels are attainable, but too often churches have installed industrial equipment only to find, too late, that it is far too noisy. Switching off the heater during the service to reduce noise is hardly ever a sensible option as the church will cool down quickly.

For a given output, forced convectors are smaller than natural convectors; they also give more control over the temperature, velocity and distribution of the warm air, which in a well-designed system can help to reduce draughts and stratification. Some design guidelines are discussed in section 6.5. Where necessary, heaters may be located remotely and the air ducted to supply and return air grilles. Filters should be fitted (and regularly maintained) to protect heat exchangers from clogging with dust and from staining, and to increase the life of decorations generally.

Discomfort, and damage to organs, etc., can sometimes be caused by hot, dry discharged air or by rapid changes in relative humidity. Discharge temperatures must not be too low or there will be draughts, and fans should be arranged to stop running if no heat is available; a low temperature cut-out is often, but not always, fitted as standard. The fans may also circulate air in summer but the improvement in comfort is usually minimal, so this feature is seldom used in practice.

Although forced warm air systems can be sized to heat a church very rapidly, care has to be taken in design. A quick blast of hot air may create an uncomfortable, stuffy environment with a high air temperature, low radiant temperatures, and cold feet. The resulting rapid changes in temperature and relative humidity may also have adverse effects on the building and its contents.

Fig. 5.8   Forced air convectors and warm air units

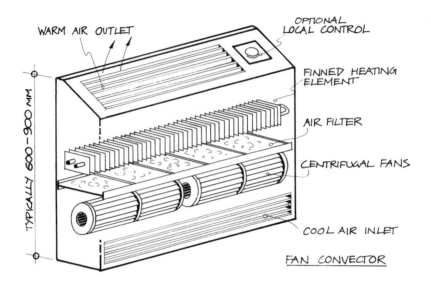

FAN CONVECTOR

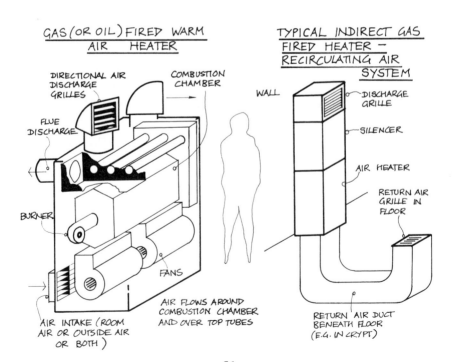

Warm air units may also be used in a more refined manner as the heat source in ducted systems: see chapter 6.

5.3.8 FAN CONVECTORS

The smaller fan-assisted units, with ratings between about 2 and 15 kilowatts, are known as fan convectors. They are most commonly heated by hot water. Gas-fired balanced flue units are also available and particularly suitable for smaller churches; one popular type has an efficiency of over 80% and a flue only 80 mm in diameter. Electric fan heaters are useful for rapid air heating in small rooms, but for larger spaces radiant heaters will normally be more effective.

Outputs are normally catalogued with fans running at high speed, but noise levels are usually only acceptable at low speed; selection must take both into account. Sometimes high fan speed is used for quicker warm-up before the church is occupied, with centralised manual or automatic change-over to low speed. With hot water systems, check that there is the boiler capacity to meet the heat demands of high speed running. Many units have integral thermostats, usually detecting return air temperature, but they can be crude and lead to wide temperature fluctuations (see chapter 7).

Air may be discharged from the top, bottom or front of fan convectors or through ductwork and diffusers. Except where used to overcome downdraughts, front or bottom discharge will help avoid stratification and project warm air towards the congregation initially. One installation discharges air through long slots at the base of the units and across the floor in a thin film; this not only keeps the warm air down but also heats up the surface of the floor before occupation. However, it requires a relatively unobstructed floor to work effectively (e.g. no hassocks).

5.4 Flueless heaters

Some gas, paraffin and light oil unit heaters are designed to discharge combustion products directly into the church. The units are relatively low in capital cost, and low running costs are claimed since no heat is lost through a flue. However, be careful as water vapour and trace chemicals in the combustion products can cause problems.

The following heat outputs produce approximately one litre of water vapour per hour:

Paraffin and bottled gas	8 kilowatts
Natural gas	7 kilowatts
Coal gas	2 kilowatts

The high production of water vapour by coal gas is one reason why, when gas lighting was common in Victorian times, more attention was given to ventilation.

Where flueless heaters are used exclusively (the odd flueless heater providing top-up in an otherwise indirectly heated church is less of a problem), the water vapour is particularly troublesome for intermittent heating. When the church is cold, internal surfaces will often be close to dew point temperature. When they come on, the heaters immediately start producing water vapour and condensation may ensue. In any event, good ventilation is essential, preferably mechanical, with extract at high level where the warmer and more humid air tends to accumulate. If nothing else, doors should be left open for an hour or so after heating to encourage the dispersal of moist air. The temptation to use a large number of heaters to provide a rapid warm-up must be resisted, particularly with radiant units, as the moisture content of the air will rise rapidly before either the air or the surfaces of many building elements are warmed. Condensation risk is reduced if units are switched on progressively, giving a gradually increasing output.

The level of other gaseous pollutants depends on the fuel burned, the burner characteristics, and the ratio of heat output to ventilation rate. Carbon dioxide and carbon monoxide concentrations must be kept below British Standard BS5990 levels of 2,800 and 10 parts per million by volume respectively; if air quality standards become even stricter, more ventilation – and the associated heat loss – might be necessary to achieve the required levels. Apart from carbon dioxide and carbon monoxide, sulphur dioxide is the major active contaminant from paraffin, and nitrogen oxides from natural gas, bottled gas producing traces of both, with possibly more oxides of nitrogen owing to higher flame temperatures. Nitrogen oxide concentrations can also increase substantially if burners are badly adjusted, particularly with bottled gas. The contaminants may do little harm under normal circumstances, but can exacerbate chemical effects of dampness and condensation. Where there are paintings, monuments, timberwork or records of particular interest within the church, expert advice should be sought.

5.5 Direct fresh air heating

A 1980s introduction from the industrial sector was the direct gas-fired fresh air heater. Fresh air is drawn into the unit, passes over the flame, and the heated air and combustion products are blown into the building together. Air flow rates are typically about 4 air changes per hour; by slightly pressurising the building with this air, draughts arising from air infiltration and natural buoyancy can often be largely eliminated. Reduced stratification is also claimed, though this requires careful design; fine adjustment of airflow and supply temperatures are critical

Fig. 5.9   **Direct fired heating**

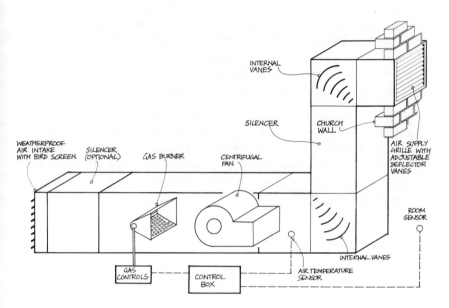

but not easily achieved in the authors' experience. For overall space heating, this technique is preferable to self-contained flueless heaters since a positive air supply is guaranteed to dilute the products of combustion.

These systems are often chosen because little equipment is visible within the church, often only a grille or two, with the rest outside at the end of a duct (see figure 5.9). They claim to provide fresh air ventilation, but this air, having been used to dilute products of combustion to statutory levels, is no longer entirely fresh. The pollutants and particularly the moisture in such air could be troublesome. There are also some worries about the effects of moisture fluctuations and trace element contaminants on items such as wall paintings and lead roofs.

Although some damp churches have been dried-out by these systems, the wetting or drying effect varies with the location; the hotter parts of the church tend to get drier and the colder ones damper. For example, in unheated vestries condensation and mould can occur unless separate background heating is provided, and moisture build-up could also take place in hidden parts of the building into which air is blown. The system is most applicable to 'uni-cellular' buildings where there are no separate closed areas.

Sometimes a rapid start may also cause condensation on cold surfaces, such as floors (which the heat tends to reach last), particularly if they are impervious and rapidly become slippery. A 'soft-start' facility, that operates the heater initially at a lower heat and moisture output can help to avoid this, but the heating needs to be started earlier. A 'post-purge' period is often included after the heating cycle to flush out the building and help remove contaminants and moisture, though it can be very uncomfortable if this operates prematurely, for example if the service is longer than expected! The effects of rapid changes in temperature and humidity, and possible moisture build-up, need to be reviewed for each application.

In a variation, the direct gas-fired heater can be replaced with one where the products of combustion are discharged through a conventional flue rather than into the heated space. The incoming fresh air is heated via a heat exchanger in the heater. Efficiencies, moisture contents, and trace element levels are all lower with such a system. In cold weather, moisture contents can be too low unless partial recirculation is used.

5.6 Local heating

For small congregations, choir practice and so on, it is unlikely to be economic to heat the whole building, however efficient the system, although some background heating is always desirable. People should either be gathered into a smaller enclosed space, such as a side-chapel, or local heating should be considered in the appropriate places, for example the chancel, the pulpit, and the front rows of pews. The aim is to produce the best local radiant temperatures with some local increase in air temperature and a minimum of draughts. Possible techniques include:

- radiant heating from overhead, using electric or gas units, or possibly an area of heated ceiling

- radiant heating from below, using an area of lightweight raised heated floor; once again there are potential safety problems if an electrically heated floor is inadvertently insulated in any way

- radiant heating from the side, possibly using local heaters in specific locations (e.g. at the lectern); another possibility is to surround the occupants as far as possible with heated screens which should come down to the floor in order to intercept cold air currents

- in some circumstances, one may be able to sweep the congregation with a gentle current of warm air from wall or floor grilles or fan-assisted heaters, although their sphere of influence will be less when used in this mode than as part of a total system.

5.7 Pew heating

Local heating may be provided for individual pews. Enclosed pews can assist such arrangements, providing protection from draughts at floor level and concealing heaters, pipes and cables.

Heaters below or behind pews may be either electric panels or tubular heaters, underpew water pipes or radiators, or areas of underfloor heating. Care must be taken not to damage the pews by the installation or the effects of the heat. Some examples are shown in figure 5.10. Systems work best where they are designed to warm the floor and the congregation as much as possible by radiation; otherwise feet become cold as the hot air convected from the units is displaced by a cold draught from elsewhere in the church. For economy, electric pew heaters with fast response may be controlled by local interval timers, the occupant of the pew pressing a button to obtain say 30 minutes' heat. Electric heaters must be carefully selected to minimise the fire hazard; in particular those which enclose the elements between plywood sheets should be avoided. All such heaters must incorporate appropriate overheat protection and be approved by the insurers. It is essential that they have BEAB (British Electrotechnical Approvals Board) approval.

Electric heaters should be protected in order to avoid singeing hassocks or burning young children's prying fingers. The insulation afforded by hassocks, etc. may also cause overheating and add to the fire hazard. Hot water pipes are likely to be safer but inflexible and difficult to alter.

Fig. 5.10 Pew heating
Cautionary notes: All electrical pew heaters must be BEAB approved
Loose hassocks should not be kept near electric pew heaters

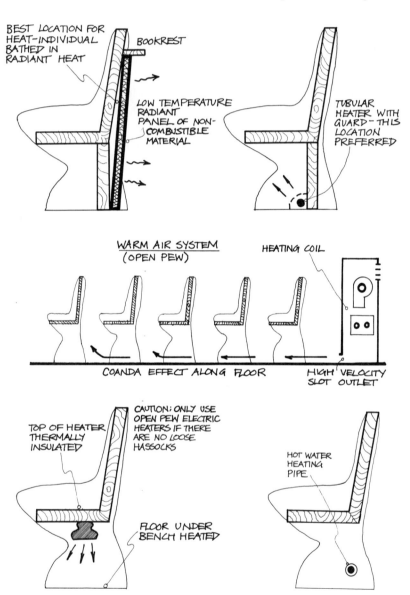

BEST LOCATION FOR HEAT-INDIVIDUAL BATHED IN RADIANT HEAT

BOOKREST

LOW TEMPERATURE RADIANT PANEL OF NON-COMBUSTIBLE MATERIAL

TUBULAR HEATER WITH GUARD – THIS LOCATION PREFERRED

WARM AIR SYSTEM (OPEN PEW)

HEATING COIL

COANDA EFFECT ALONG FLOOR

HIGH VELOCITY SLOT OUTLET

TOP OF HEATER THERMALLY INSULATED

CAUTION; ONLY USE OPEN PEW ELECTRIC HEATERS IF THERE ARE NO LOOSE HASSOCKS

HOT WATER HEATING PIPE

FLOOR UNDER BENCH HEATED

OPEN PEW SOLUTIONS

6

Central heating

With central heating, heat generated in one place is distributed by means of air or hot water to local heat emitters. Steam is now little used and will not be discussed further. Details of equipment and systems may be found in standard texts, for example Faber and Kell (see further reading, listed under Martin P.L. and Oughton D.R.).

It is easy to regard central heating as the ideal, but alternatives may be more effective and cheaper to run, particularly in intermittently-used buildings. Central heating originated when coal-firing was universal. It then had a number of advantages. In figure 6.1 these are compared with the present day where there are more alternatives. Nevertheless, central heating has its attractions, not least in keeping fuel-burning equipment out of the church itself. Systems need to be carefully controlled in order to avoid waste, particularly when the pattern of use in different parts of the building varies greatly. Central heating is better suited to more continuously used buildings, where underfloor and warm air systems may be considered for new projects and major refurbishments.

Many churches have elderly central heating systems which are ineffective and expensive to run. The choice is often between overhaul or complete replacement. Replacement will often bring better comfort with lower running costs, though sometimes the existing system may be retained for background heating during cold weather.

Central systems often have advantages in safety, longevity, fuel flexibility and localisation of fuel-burning plant. However, in intermittently used churches they can be more expensive to run owing to slow response times, lack of flexibility and distribution losses. Particular problems arise where:

- the system heats a number of spaces simultaneously, often using the same controls, while only some of the spaces are in use: 'zones' of substantially different requirements should always have independent time and temperature controls.

- only a small amount of heat is required: in warmer weather, when only a small area is in use, or for domestic hot water, the whole system has to be activated. Even where zone control is good, circulation losses and poor low load boiler efficiencies can often reduce overall thermal efficiencies from 70% or so to 30% or less.

Once there is central heating, it is tempting to use the plant for all heating needs on the site. This made sense where coal-fired plant was fired continuously but with modern equipment it can be inefficient. Unit heaters or even perhaps a small domestic central heating system may be best for other scattered uses. Domestic hot water is a common offender: large tanks and circulating pipework are kept hot (often too hot) for long periods in order to meet an occasional need. Standards for storage and circulation temperatures are laid down to minimise the risks from *legionella* bacteria. Independent hot water systems should always be considered very seriously, even where there is a central system already; if demands are small or infrequent, local electric or gas water heaters can be very cost-effective, provided they are manually or automatically switched-off when not required.

6.1   Wet systems

Systems distributing heat by hot water are of three types: high, medium and low pressure. For reasons of safety and simplicity, low pressure hot water (LPHW) systems now predominate.

In LPHW systems the water is below atmospheric boiling point and normally leaves the boiler room at about 80°C (180°F), returning at about 70°C (160°F) or sometimes 60°C once the system is warmed-up. For floor heating, and where heat pumps are used, flow temperatures are usually lower, between 40° and 60°C. Condensing boilers also become more efficient at lower return temperatures.

Originally circulation was by gravity, which required large pipes carefully laid out so that the warm water rose away from the boiler. Steady circulation took a long time to be established, but this did not much matter with coal firing where the boiler seldom went out. The boiler was normally in a basement or underground chamber to improve the circulation head. Such chambers sometimes flood and their suitability for any new equipment should be carefully reviewed.

Today pumped circulation is universal, and nearly all gravity systems have had booster (accelerator) pumps added. Pumped circulation allows:

- a faster response

- positive water circulation independent of temperature

- smaller, higher resistance pipes, boilers and heat emitters, simplifying installation and reducing capital cost

- greater flexibility in boiler location and in pipe layout.

Fig. 6.1   Technical aspects of central heating

Early advantages of central heating	Present day situation
Plant and messy coal and ash handling restricted to a single location.	Central plant is convenient for operation and maintenance, and alterations are possible centrally without affecting the installation elsewhere, giving some flexibility to adapt to changes in fuel availability and price.
Space-consuming and intrusive stoves, fireplaces and flues taken out of the building.	Modern unit equipment is more compact and less intrusive than its predecessors, though noise levels need checking; flues, even compact advanced designs, can be difficult to accommodate and a single location will often be preferable.
Higher thermal efficiency than stoves and open fires.	The peak thermal efficiencies of modern unit heaters often differ little from central plant.
Greater controllability than stoves and open fires.	Controls for all types of heating system are now much improved; central systems may lack some flexibility in operation.
Lower capital costs.	Mass-produced and easily fitted units often cost less installed than the more tailor-made central systems.
Lower maintenance costs.	Central systems are normally longer-lived than units, with fewer parts requiring regular maintenance; however, unit heaters are more simply maintained, parts are standardised and may be kept in stock, and whole units may be replaced individually if necessary.
Reduced fire risk.	The increased fire risk with unit equipment remains, although substantially mitigated now through improvements in standards of manufacture, design, installation and safety systems.

Fig. 6.2   Hot water central heating schematics

Upper diagram: Typical older system: modern systems may differ slightly

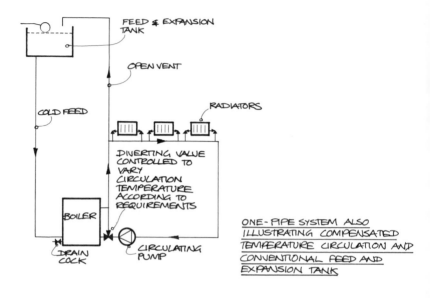

ONE-PIPE SYSTEM ALSO
ILLUSTRATING COMPENSATED
TEMPERATURE CIRCULATION AND
CONVENTIONAL FEED AND
EXPANSION TANK

TWO-PIPE SYSTEM ALSO
ILLUSTRATING CONSTANT
TEMPERATURE CIRCULATION
AND PRESSURIZATION
UNIT

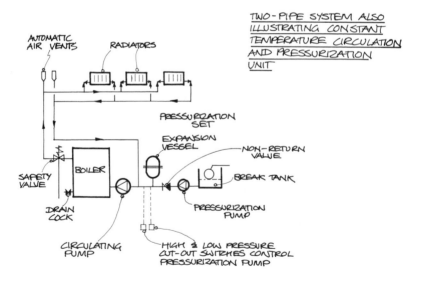

Pumped circulation through existing gravity systems can cause problems. More rapid temperature changes place old pipework and joints under increased thermal stress, which can lead to failure, and may dislodge sludge, causing blockages.

Circulation systems are of two main types: one-pipe and two-pipe (figure 6.2). In today's more common two-pipe system, each heat emitter bridges between flow and return pipes, and receives hot water directly from the boiler.

In the two-pipe system, sizing is simplified and more positive circulation obtained through each heat emitter. This is particularly important with high-efficiency natural and fan convector units, which have small internal waterways and a high hydraulic resistance. In the older one-pipe design, each radiator returns hot water to the pipe it came from, so there is a temperature drop down the pipe, requiring radiator sizes to be graded. Modified one-pipe systems are also used, in which diverting radiator valves ensure a positive water flow through each heat emitter when required.

Conventional low pressure hot water systems require a feed and expansion tank above the highest point in the system; this can be difficult to locate in a church and to protect from frost. Small mechanical pressurisation units are now often used as an alternative, usually located in the boiler room (figure 6.2).

Circulation pipes should always be well insulated where they do not provide useful heat directly to the relevant spaces. Old insulation of pipes and boilers may contain asbestos and could be a health hazard. If there is any doubt, get it tested and if necessary encapsulated or removed by specialists.

Pipes outside the heated space and through which heated water does not circulate (for example, water pipes and pipes to feed and expansion vessels) should be well insulated and possibly separately heated by electric heating tape when there is a frost risk.

6.2 Boilers

The heat source for wet systems is known as a boiler, although only in steam systems does the water actually boil. Boilers generally have two parts: the combustion chamber, and convection sections where heat is extracted from the gaseous combustion products. Many old boilers and some modern stoves have no convection section at all but these are needlessly inefficient by today's standards.

For fuel economy, it is important to select boilers of high efficiency. Efficiencies are normally quoted at full rated output and until recently were in the range 70-85% of the gross calorific value of the fuel, with the practical upper limit occurring when water vapour and chemicals from the combustion products condensed and corroded the boiler and flue. Modern gas- and oil-fired boilers now tend to have efficiencies of 80% or more, with condensing boilers around 90%. Care should be taken in comparing efficiencies: the nett calorific value is sometimes quoted and gives more impressive-looking figures.

Condensing boilers have an additional or supplementary corrosion-resistant convection section in which the flue gases are cooled until the water vapour within them may actually condense. These have a higher efficiency but require special chimney construction and a drain connection for the condensate (figure 6.3).

For systems where the return water temperature is low (55°C), there may be extra advantages in using a condensing boiler. This situation can occur if the system is being used for background heating. For large churches there are benefits in installing a multi-boiler system in which the first one to operate is a condensing boiler. This reduces the capital cost while retaining most of the benefits of condensing plant.

Care must be taken in the design of a boiler system to ensure that minimum water flow rates are maintained through the boiler under all conditions. Low water flow rates cause excessive temperature rises and can result in premature failure due to thermal stressing. In most systems it is also important to include 'pump over-run' to ensure that residual heat in the system is dispersed.

Fig. 6.3   Condensing boiler

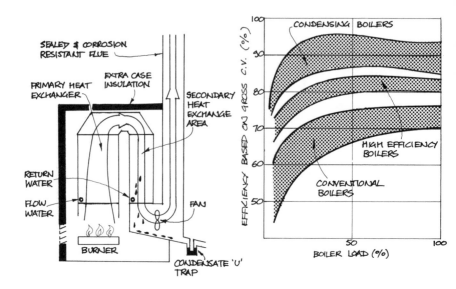

A boiler which is efficient at full rating will not necessarily be efficient on a particular system. Part-load boiler efficiency is usually, although not invariably, worse than at peak output; system efficiency almost inevitably is, as equipment and distribution systems are kept warm but not fully stretched. Situations where boilers and systems are on light duty should be avoided through design, operation and control. Where they are inevitable, either boilers with good part-load characteristics (e.g. condensing boilers) should be selected, or the load should be split between several boilers, with suitable sequence controls, correctly commissioned (see chapter 7).

Boilers are generally located in their own rooms, normally to meet regulations, and to reduce problems of noise, safety and intrusion. The boiler room should be adequate in size, dry and not prone to flooding, well-ventilated and with good access; it should be used only for the equipment it contains, and not as a dump. If these requirements are ignored (and they often are!) the result will be poor maintenance, reduced life and efficiency, and increased safety and fire hazards.

The traditional heating boiler, assembled from cast iron sections, is relatively large and heavy. Suitable locations are restricted; if foundations are not sound the castings may crack. Although often quite efficient under sustained full and part-loads, their mass and large water content gives them a slow thermal response which makes them better suited to continuous heating applications.

Most boilers are now fabricated from steel, copper or light iron castings; they are generally more compact and convenient. Peak efficiencies are similar to well-designed and maintained sectional boilers, and, on a year-round basis, efficiencies are often higher, owing to faster response to demand. The life of fabricated boilers, typically 15 to 20 years, is generally shorter than sectional ones, but this is often compensated by lower purchase, installation and running costs. The units are however more likely to fail if system design or operation is faulty. Infrequent operation of any boiler does not necessarily prolong its life, since damage is caused by thermal stresses, condensation and corrosion.

In commercial and industrial installations, it is common to split the load between two or more boilers; this provides standby capacity for maintenance and breakdown, and gives a better load match between boiler output and heating demand in milder weather. This duplication will probably be extravagant in the smaller and intermittently-heated church, but is worthwhile for larger and more continuously operated installations. A more recent development is to use a larger number of identical small modular gas or oil boilers. These can simplify installation where space is restricted, and allow improved fuel efficiencies at part loads, provided they are properly controlled. Effective control however needs care in design, commissioning and maintenance.

6.3 District or group heating

Occasionally hot water will be available from site mains serving an area or a group of buildings. Rates for heat supply may be competitive, particularly if the need not to purchase, operate and maintain boilers is taken into account. However, the prospect of potentially cheap heat should not override other considerations in system selection. Occasionally churches are offered very low flat rates which it would be silly to refuse provided the contract runs for a reasonable time. However, as a matter of principle it is usually preferable to pay for the heat actually used or waste and higher costs will eventually be inevitable.

6.4 Re-use of old systems

Old hot water heating systems may often be in a sound condition, with the exception of the boiler, pump and control: should they be replaced? The answer depends largely on how effective they were in the first place, and whether it is desirable to retain a hot water system as background or full central heating.

If the answer is yes, or probably yes, to both questions, the system should be checked in detail. This would involve:

- a visual inspection of all heat emitters and pipework

- a careful inspection of all joints and joint systems

- pressure test of the system

- draining down and chemical test of water in the system

- internal inspection of typical lengths of pipework: this can now often be done non-destructively with fibre optics, intrascopes, etc.

If these checks are satisfactory, the system would need to be thoroughly flushed out, cleaned externally and have any defective parts replaced. Specialist advice should be obtained on suitable chemical treatment for the water in the system: this applies to newer systems as well. Chemical cleaning can do more harm than good! Alterations to the existing system should otherwise be kept to a minimum, as they may disturb sound parts of the installation; if more heat emitters are required, they should normally be on a separate circuit. The boiler size will also need review to ensure sufficient capacity. Any heat emitters added to the original circuit should have large waterways similar to the originals. Modern high-efficiency natural and fan convectors will not obtain sufficient circulation and some types may be prone to blockage if any remaining sludge is dislodged, as may the waterways in modern low water content boilers and motorised valves; strainers and sumps are advisable.

Many old systems were intended for continuous coal firing and lower internal temperatures than today: their large water content and limited heating surface thus make them slow-responding and generally unsuitable for occasional heating needs. Large diameter cast iron pipes with caulked joints may have lasted for nearly a century, but modern pumps and boilers may subject them to rapid temperature fluctuations which can cause leaks and cracks. Older systems are therefore most appropriate for background heating, coupled to a small boiler, preferably condensing, or possibly a heat pump.

6.5   Warm air systems

Warm air systems are less common in the UK in general, and in churches in particular. The size of ducts required and the location requirements for diffusers generally restrict sensitive applications to new buildings and to major alteration works. Careful design is required to control noise levels: see section 8.2.

As with water systems, the earlier types used gravity circulation by natural buoyancy, while today forced fan-assisted circulation is standard. Gravity systems are occasionally found, often with hot air stoves in pits under the floor: they usually cause draughts, stains and bad stratification, and are best replaced. Their flues may have long horizontal runs and be unsafe, particularly where intermittent use no longer allows a good draught to be established. It may be possible to use the ducts as part of a new hot water or forced warm air system.

Forced air systems use an air heat exchanger in place of the waterways in a boiler and a fan in place of the pump. Sometimes flueless firing is used. Fuel-burning air heaters should preferably be in fire-resistant compartments (for larger units these may be statutorily necessary), and ductwork requires fire dampers where it passes between compartments. In order to reduce duct sizes a number of heaters are often used; these may alternatively have hot water heating coils, supplied from a central boiler plant, a system which increases controllability and reduces noise problems and fire risks. Good frost protection arrangements for fresh air heater coils are vital.

Forced air systems in churches are often poor, with a single unit heater blasting out hot air noisily and indiscriminately. Good systems are also possible, especially in new buildings, where air is carefully diffused throughout the church to give a fast warm-up, good temperature distribution and avoidance of draughts and stratification. If air is introduced into the church above 35-40°C, stratification is almost inevitable unless air distribution is very carefully considered.

Air flow in ducted systems has to be carefully balanced between the outlets to ensure effective heat distribution. Ductwork should be leaktight and insulated.

Fig. 6.4   Warm air systems

Caution: temperatures at roof apex are not always high – check before installing.

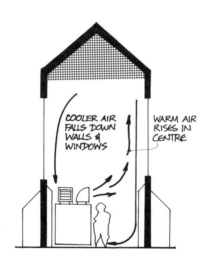

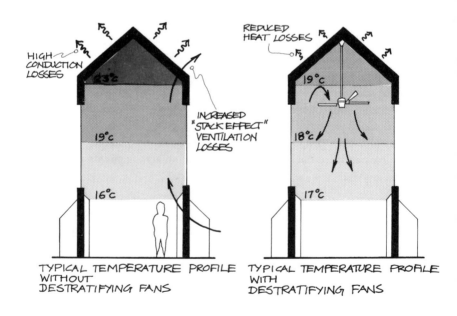

Where fresh air is introduced through the system the volume and any controls need to be carefully set up and regularly checked. Too much outside air will lead to dryness and high fuel use, too little could result in high relative humidities.

7

Controls

Automatic controls are essential to improve performance and avoid waste but they must be correctly selected, located, connected and calibrated in the first place. A number of devices and methods discussed in this chapter may be found only in older installations and, whilst they may continue to work, it will often be worth replacing them. With recent developments, particularly in electronics, major advances on traditional practice are now possible at low cost. Accurate control of boilers and room temperatures with central heating is particularly important: a lot of energy can otherwise be wasted.

Controls are the vital connection between the user and the system. They should be correctly located, simple to operate and easy to understand; if they are too complicated or difficult to reach or to see, they can easily be ignored. A time switch is unlikely to be set sensibly if it is in a locked metal cabinet full of mysterious electrical equipment in a dirty subterranean boiler chamber. Equally, nothing is entirely automatic; successful operation ultimately relies on someone checking and making adjustments to match the performance of the system most economically to the requirements. Simple operating procedures and checks should be posted alongside any controls which need to be adjusted.

Communal buildings such as churches need most controls to be tamperproof, so that only the persons specifically charged with looking after the system, be they churchwarden, outside specialist or maintenance company, can change settings and make adjustments. The exception is for local over-ride controls, which people should be able to switch locally when required (e.g. pew heating or in a chapel). Some systems switch off automatically after a given interval of, say 30 minutes or 1 hour, if not manually switched off before then.

For convenience, controls are considered in four groups: safety, time, capacity, and temperature.

7.1   Safety controls

Safety controls are essential to avoid danger if systems fail in some way, particularly through overheating, escape of unburnt fuel, or failure of electrical equipment. Safety devices are normally supplied as an integral part of 'packaged' boilers and heaters. They will include a high temperature cut-out, a flame failure device where appropriate, and interlocks between logically connected operations (e.g. fan to run before fuel can be supplied to a forced draught burner).

Church heating will often operate when there is nobody present, or even close by, and additional protection will usually be necessary. For instance:

- some high temperature cut-outs reset automatically; this is not advisable since faults may persist undetected

- in hot water central heating systems, a flow switch should be fitted to stop the boiler firing if water flow is interrupted; this is essential for low water content boilers; warm air units should also have a similar device in the air stream

- a fusible link and automatic fuel cut-off fire valve should be considered as a final fail-safe on high-rated equipment, even where not statutorily necessary (e.g. for gas boilers). If possible the fire valve should be at the fuel tank outlet or the point of entry to the boiler room, with a clearly identified quick-release at the door.

Boilers should also be equipped with a safety valve, a pressure gauge, and thermometers for flow, return and flue gas temperatures. Further safety devices and controls may be fitted if the situation is thought to merit them. For instance, a float switch may be fitted in a tank (e.g. a water feed and expansion tank) to switch off the system and give an audible or visible warning if the water level is low or if it overflows. The correct operation of these devices should be checked regularly.

Wet central heating systems need to be protected from frost regardless of all other control settings. The simplest method uses a carefully placed and accurate (preferably electronic or mercury) room thermostat to start the system if the internal temperature falls below say 5°C. If conservation heating is employed, then a higher temperature, say 10°C, may be preferred. Some modern equipment uses the same sensor for room temperature control and for frost protection. The more common and cheaper bi-metallic thermostats are generally less precise and, unless set high (when they may bring the heating on unnecessarily), they may not protect the system reliably. An accurate external thermostat, commonly known as a frost-stat, may also be used. This may be set to a lower temperature, perhaps 2° or 3°C, and start the circulating pumps only. If the return water temperature or the room temperature then falls below a low pre-set limit, the boiler is fired. Care must be taken to avoid prolonged periods of intermittent firing at low circulating temperatures which can cause corrosion within boilers not designed to be condensing.

Frost protection systems should be checked from time to time, to make sure that they work and also that they do not bring the heating on needlessly when there is no freezing risk. A maximum and minimum thermometer in the church, or an hours-run timer on the frost protection circuit, will provide useful checks on what has been happening.

7.2   Time controls

All systems will benefit from time controls, if only to switch everything on and off as necessary. More elaborate versions can programme equipment, space and circulation temperatures for different periods. The selection and location of time controls requires a degree of care and thought which, sadly, it seldom receives. For instance, many churches have domestic time switches designed to repeat the same programme every 24 hours. A widely-used commercial timer allows whole days (e.g. Monday to Saturday) to be omitted from the programme, but it is difficult to set and not particularly well suited to varying uses and heating needs during the week. A daily programme also does not permit extended warm up times when necessary. The result is that although the heating could have come on at, say 11 p.m. on Saturday evening, it is switched on earlier manually at the convenience of the person responsible. Many time controls are also inconveniently located, difficult to see and difficult to set, and are thus incorrectly used or bypassed altogether. Clock hands or a digital time display (provided it is well-lit and easy to read!) are useful aids to correct setting.

A 7-day time switch is normally the simplest appropriate type. The settings can be changed at any time, but frequently it will be convenient to establish a routine. Some time switches can cover an entire month's programme, but the mechanical ones may have very coarse control settings, whilst the electronic ones can be more difficult to set than the 7-day units. Check that you are happy with the choice of unit.

Electronic time controls permit more accurate and sophisticated programming than an electromechanical time switch, and can often programme a number of devices from the one unit. With some products a programme may be established for the entire year, taking account of events at regular weekly, monthly or quarterly intervals, and also permitting ad hoc instructions which are 'forgotten' once they have been executed. This sounds ideal, but it requires skill to set up and the programme is not normally displayed all at once: units often have to be 'interrogated', a process which many people find irritating and confusing.

Units with automatic clockwork or battery reserves must be specified to avoid the need to reset every time the electrical supply is interrupted. An extended reserve period with a fast recovery time may be needed where the electricity is habitually switched off when the church is not in use. However, switching off supplies to heating controls is not recommended, particularly for wet systems, because frost protection facilities would be lost; electrical distribution boards and isolating switches should be arranged accordingly.

Time controls should be located in a convenient position, but where they cannot be interfered with by unauthorised people, for example in a locked box by the door, or in the vestry. Before selecting any particular control make sure that the person who will adjust it understands it and considers it convenient to use. Controls requiring regular adjustment should not normally be put inside equipment control panels, as this makes people unwilling to use them.

Heating for special occasions is often most easily dealt with by independent time-limited over-ride switches. These are simple to install and use, and give heating for a predetermined time, after which the system switches off again.

7.2.1   OPTIMUM START TIMERS

Since the warm-up time of a building varies with outside temperature, sun and wind conditions, and the internal starting temperature, fixed time controls are not ideal, especially for slow-responding systems and buildings. Equally, the thermal capacity of a massive building may permit the heating to be switched off before occupancy ceases. Optimum start/stop controls do this automatically and are worth considering, particularly for wet central heating systems in regular daily use, and are mandatory on new systems over 100 kW.

The optimum start process is outlined in figure 7.1. The controller requires internal and external temperature sensors and is set like a time switch, but only to the periods during which the church will actually be occupied. It then calculates the necessary warm-up time and starts the system accordingly. Some units require calibration by the installer; others monitor the building's warm-up characteristics and calibrate themselves, at least in theory - their correct operation needs to be checked. Optimum start can give improved performance and saves heating fuel in mild weather but, when it is cold, the heating may run for longer. In order to avoid excessive preheat periods, the earliest allowable start time may be entered on most units. Performance needs to be checked from time to time, to see that running hours are as expected - a poorly-set optimiser can waste more fuel than it was intended to save! Some controllers can also show the time at which they started the heating, and when they intend to stop it.

Full optimum start facilities are rarely worthwhile in many churches but simplified forms can be effective. Such devices can measure the temperature and determine an appropriate delay before starting the heating system. If the building is already quite warm, the heating will start later than when it is colder. With this type of control the programming of heating for intermittent use is particularly easy.

7.2.2   PUMP RUN-ON TIMERS

With many wet heating systems, particularly the older ones with 4-inch pipes and cast-iron boilers, much heat is stored bringing the boiler and distribution pipework up to temperature. The boiler should thus be turned off before the end of the heating period, while the pump continues running to prevent overshoot of the boiler temperature and to dissipate stored heat effectively into the building. This is normally achieved either by a 'run-on' timer or by a thermostat which keeps the pump running until the water temperature has dropped to a pre-set level.

7.3   Capacity controls

Capacity controls regulate heat input or output in accordance with estimated requirements. The most common types are input controllers, sequence controllers and compensated controllers.

Input controllers are used with heat storage systems, such as electric night storage heaters and floor heating, to avoid too much heat being put into store: they are particularly necessary with intermittent use, since any excess will be wasted when nobody is there. The simplest controller relates the charge merely to the prevailing external temperature; more sophisticated ones take account of the inside temperature and of the period over which heat is required for the coming day.

Sequence controllers: many boilers are most efficient when operating continuously at full output. They are sized, however, to meet a peak requirement which obtains for only a small part of the year (figure 7.2).

During milder weather it may be best to restrict the number of boilers or heaters in operation. In a church, manual sequencing is normally sufficient. In a larger building in more frequent use, automatic sequence control should be used, and is mandatory on new installations over 100 kW. For these controls to work effectively, care needs to be taken in the design of boiler pipework and valves, and in specifying and commissioning the controls.

Compensated controllers (figure 7.3): for systems which have the capacity to heat the building well, and in buildings which are heated daily, the maximum

Fig. 7.1   Optimum start control

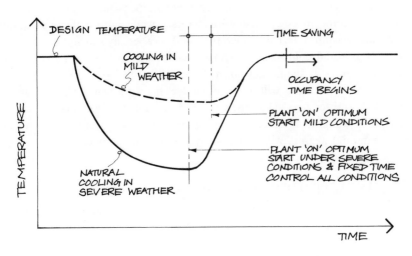

Fig. 7.2   Heating S-curve for a typical boiler system

Fig. 7.3   Typical compensated control

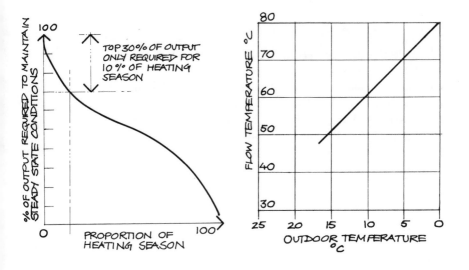

available output from wet central heating can be limited by using a 'compensator' to alter the circulating water temperature. Simple compensators reduce circulation temperatures as the outside temperature increases, while more sophisticated units also take into account internal temperatures and occasionally sun and wind conditions. Compensated control is particularly useful with hot water radiators and radiant convectors. It should not normally be applied to forced air and fan convector systems or draughts will result, and it does not work as well where different types of heat emitter are used on the same water circuit. It is best if compensation is overridden while the building is warming up. Otherwise, lower circulation temperatures in mild weather will extend the pre-heat period unnecessarily.

7.4   Temperature controls

Many church heating systems are only operated *in extremis* and space temperature limiting control may appear ludicrous. Nevertheless, overheating and excess running times commonly occur, particularly in milder weather.

Warm air and fan convector heaters often have integral controls which detect the temperature of room air returning to the unit; these are often limited in accuracy and in consistency. Central or group control is often preferable. Fan convectors can usefully be controlled by two-stage thermostats to run them at high speed for warm-up, dropping to a quieter lower speed during services. Automatic progressive reduction of fan speed as the temperature rises is also an effective means of control in some cases.

Thermostatic radiator valves (TRVs) are an effective low-cost method of controlling hot water radiators and convectors, but very few are suitable for existing one-pipe systems. They are particularly useful for heaters in smaller rooms attached to a central system. For large spaces with many heat emitters, an air thermostat to control the boiler or a motorised valve is often preferable. The sensing heads of TRVs should be installed where they are not affected by heat from the emitters or from the connecting pipework; valves with remote sensors or setting dials may be used where necessary. In public areas, setting heads with robust tamperproof guards should normally be specified to avoid damage and unauthorised adjustment. In private rooms a click-stop at the preferred position gives a useful reminder and makes re-setting easy.

Some hot water convectors are controlled by dampers in the air stream. These are often rather crude and ineffective and TRVs on the water side are preferable.

Domestic room thermostats with open dials and bi-metallic or capsule elements are often used in churches. However:

- tamperproof versions should normally be selected

- the cheaper versions can have a wide temperature differential between switching off and coming on, which causes discomfort and energy waste, particularly with warm air heating

- where 'accelerator heaters' are fitted to speed up response times, a fixed setting tends to give slightly higher air temperatures in mild weather than when it is colder, while the opposite behaviour will usually be more comfortable and economical.

High-accuracy electronic temperature sensors, although more expensive, should be seriously considered, particularly for large areas and for frost protection. Adjustment should be easy but tampering by unauthorised persons should be discouraged; with electronic controls the dial may be separate from the sensor, perhaps beside the time controls. Some products may be programmed to achieve different space temperatures for different time periods.

It can be difficult to choose a good location for a temperature sensor or thermostat. On an outside wall, it is affected by heat loss and thermal capacity of the structure, while beneath a window it may suffer from downdraughts or heat rising from pipes below, or sometimes from the sun shining on it! A good place is often on a lightweight screen or furnishing away from windows and heat emitters. In a larger installation, several detectors may be installed and suitable combinations employed; for instance, controlling from the maximum, minimum or average of a number of readings.

With radiant heating it is best to use thermostats which respond to both radiant and air temperatures. Siting these sensors is critical and should be discussed carefully with manufacturers and designers.

With central heating, compensated controls may be supplemented with room thermostats and thermostatic radiator valves to avoid local overheating. When a number of differently-used spaces (e.g. a church and church hall) are heated by the same installation, independent time and temperature controls for each space are essential. These would generally open a motorised valve to the zone when heat is required and only energise the boiler when one or more of the valves was open.

7.5   Adjustment and commissioning

It is unwise to assume that controls will function faultlessly the first time: it is all too common for them to be connected incorrectly if at all! Proving tests should be specified and witnessed by a client representative and the results recorded. On the larger and more complex systems, the appointment of an independent commissioning engineer should be seriously considered. Subsequent maintenance should include checks on the operation and calibration of the controls.

8

Environmental and operating considerations

This chapter is concerned with operating and maintaining existing and new systems to give the best performance with minimum fuel use. It also deals with relatively low-cost methods of upgrading existing installations. Although it is commonly felt that churches cost too much to heat, in relation to their volume much less is normally spent than on other building types. The problem of getting maximum benefit for minimum outlay is nevertheless very real and is also important from the environmental standpoint. Improving the heating system not only helps the treasurer but also contributes to the reduction of fuel usage which will become increasingly necessary.

All heating systems require care and attention to operate satisfactorily, safely and economically, and arrangements should be made for this to happen. The fuel consumption should also be checked at regular intervals: it is much better to have advance warning than to be confronted by a large bill. Inappropriate design, installation and control features will often be identified and be worth rectifying. For intermittently-occupied churches, attention to the heating system and its controls will nearly always be more cost-effective than improving the building's insulation.

8.1   Operation and maintenance

Too often heating systems are taken for granted until they go wrong. The result is that equipment goes out of tune and develops undetected faults, control settings become inappropriate, performance deteriorates and fuel consumption increases. When faults finally become apparent, some damage may have been done, increasing repair costs.

The best solution is to make an interested, capable and committed person responsible for the operation and maintenance of the system and for monitoring its fuel consumption. It may be appropriate to provide some training. This does not mean such people should carry out technical inspections and clean the burners themselves, but maintenance contractors are unlikely to keep up to the mark unless someone keeps an eye on their work, draws attention to shortcomings, checks the bills and thanks them when the job has been well done. Contractors also cannot be expected to know as much about the detailed pattern of use of the church and the perceived performance of the heating as those who use the church regularly; and they will be inclined to set controls generously to avoid call-backs.

The duties of the person responsible should include:

- having a good overall knowledge of any heating, ventilation and humidity control systems

- being aware of the way in which the systems can be made to operate most effectively, particularly through switching equipment off entirely at times when it is unlikely to be needed

- knowing the detailed pattern of use of the church and making sure that the controls are set to meet the comfort requirements effectively, but without waste

- checking the operation of the system (e.g. time switching, valve operation, flame characteristics, circulation and flue gas temperatures) occasionally to make sure that all is well

- monitoring space temperatures and humidities from time to time to check the performance of the system (e.g. to reduce thermostat and time settings, particularly in milder weather), and to be aware of possible dangers to the building fabric and its contents

- arranging for maintenance, and checking that it has been properly carried out.

Simple monitoring devices should also be available, particularly:

- a maximum and minimum thermometer

- a simple hygrometer

- for central heating boilers and the larger air heaters, thermometers showing flow, return and flue gas temperatures.

A wet and dry bulb whirling hygrometer or equivalent electronic instrument is also useful for more accurate spot checks, provided it is properly calibrated and used. Records of readings can be invaluable to advisers if problems occur or if alterations to the building or the heating are being considered. Where problems are detected, more sophisticated recording equipment (such as a thermohygrograph or its electronic equivalent) may be borrowed or hired. Electronic data logging equipment is now common and increasingly cost-effective and should be considered for longer term detailed checks.

Arrangements should be made for boilers, burners, flues, pumps, fans and controls to be checked thoroughly at least once a year and heat emitters cleaned from time to time. Chemical tests and water treatment may also be necessary. The work needs to be carefully specified and supervised. Combustion efficiency tests and burner adjustments should be made regularly, particularly with oil and forced draught gas burners. Chimney cleaning should not be forgotten, particularly with solid fuel equipment; where wood and waste products are burned, this may be several times a year.

8.2   Noise

Required noise levels should be carefully considered and specified. They are more exacting in larger churches and where sound recording and broadcasting are carried out. The subject of acoustics is specialised, and advice should be sought.

There are several variables to be considered:

- external noise: in some situations background noise, for example from passing traffic, can exceed any internally generated sound from a heating system

- audibility within the church: this depends not only on background sound levels but on the acoustics of the building and the nature of any sound reinforcing equipment; it is also a function of the frequency range of both the sounds which are desired and the background sound

- the size of the building: larger buildings generally require quieter heating systems

- any requirements for regular or occasional broadcasting from the church.

Any air movement will generate some noise but by careful design and equipment selection (if necessary including silencers), this can often be reduced to levels which are acceptable for the particular circumstances and use of the building. Noise levels of 35 dBA (or NR30) can usually be achieved in the centre of churches with reasonable measures but in a smaller church 45 dBA may be good enough. Levels below 35 dBA normally require considerable care and expense.

On occasions noise breakout from one area to another can be a problem. Even if equipment gives acceptable sound levels within the church, externally mounted units, air intakes and flues can occasionally cause a nuisance to neighbours.

8.3   Monitoring fuel consumption

Fuel costs are too often greeted with resigned acceptance, or a prayer that things will be better next season. However, excess fuel consumption is a useful symptom of something wrong: a faulty control, poor burner adjustment, ventilators left open, or a time switch or thermostat changed to meet some unusual requirement and not re-set. Once a review procedure is established, monitoring fuel use against targets is a quick, simple and effective method of managing expenditure and ensuring optimum plant performance.

Records are usually kept of the cost of fuel used, but not the amount. Meter readings should be taken preferably at weekly and certainly at monthly intervals: a quarterly bill is too long after the event. With stored fuel such as oil, delivery records are a poor indication of the fuel burned; more exact measurement is best, preferably by meter which also helps to avoid fraud.

Where main gas and electricity meters supply a number of locations, sub-meters on the supplies to the church are desirable. An hour-run meter on the burner circuit is also a worthwhile check on its intensity of use.

Fig. 8.1   Fuel consumption

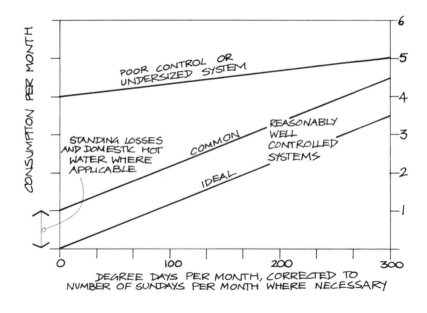

Plant performance may be reviewed by plotting the fuel used each month against average outside temperature or 'Degree Days' (regional figures are available from the Department of the Environment and local figures may be obtained from the Meteorological Office and other sources). Figure 8.1 illustrates relationships commonly obtained.

In some instances, the consumption curves will indicate a need for alterations. For instance, relatively high summertime consumption often arises where heating boilers also provide domestic hot water; it will often be better to arrange some other form of water heating and switch the boilers off. If fuel consumption is only loosely dependent on outside temperatures, then either the system is grossly undersized or ineffectively controlled, and modifications are desirable.

Whether alterations are made or not, a knowledge of the past performance of the plant allows the likely future fuel use to be predicted, using temperature or degree-day figures for average years. By comparing this with the actual monthly figures, early warning of problems may be obtained and the value of energy-saving measures may be evaluated. For instance, an increase in fuel consumption from year to year could indicate faulty or badly-maintained equipment, a loss of interest in operating the system and setting controls effectively, or increasing use of the church.

There are several rules of thumb which have been suggested as yardsticks for energy performance of churches. One such, for churches in weekend use, suggests the following levels of annual heating energy consumption per cubic metre of heated volume:

$5\text{-}10 \text{ kWh/m}^3$	The church is either underheated or makes good use of local or fast-responding heating.
$10\text{-}15 \text{ kWh/m}^3$	This range is common for large churches with all types of heating and small churches with unit space heating.
$15\text{-}20 \text{ kWh/m}^3$	This range is common for small churches with central heating, and churches generally, where reasonable comfort conditions are attempted with older central heating systems sized for continuous use and with insufficient capacity to permit a reasonably fast warm-up.

The figures compare with $50\text{-}100 \text{ kWh/m}^3$ per annum for other building types such as houses, schools and offices, and for churches in regular daily use. For a given type of system the consumption index will tend to be higher for the small church, which has a proportionately greater heat loss, and where controls are usually less sophisticated than in larger installations.

Another yardstick has been produced by the Environment and Energy Management Directorate based on square metres of floor area. This suggests energy efficiency ratings for churches with weekend and occasional weekday use as follows:

Fossil fuel less than 80 kWh/m² per year, plus electricity less than 10 kWh/m² per year	Good: churches with local or fast-responding heating systems should fall into this category
Fossil fuel less than 150 kWh/m² per year, plus electricity less than 20 kWh/m² per year	Fair: church probably has reasonable controls and procedures, but significant savings should be possible
More than the above	Poor: urgent action probably needed, unless there are special reasons for the high consumption, for example, regular daily use

More detailed performance criteria have been suggested by Marks in his book, *Heat and Light*. He takes account of the amount of usage of the building as well as its type of heating. His calculations are based on a Weekly Heated Volume (WHV) which is then multiplied by a factor according to the type of heating system employed to give a target maximum annual consumption for the particular church or church complex. Since this work originates from Scottish experience it may require adaptation for use with the milder climate further south.

8.4 Improving energy efficiency

The objective is to make more effective use of the fuel which is being consumed or, in other words, to obtain more useful heat per pound spent. Most efforts to improve heating system efficiency and to reduce building heat loss will be successful to some degree, though not always saving energy. Sometimes performance and comfort will be improved instead. In selecting the most cost-effective measures, the normal order of priority is:

- good management: maintaining equipment properly, reviewing standards and scheduling the use of spaces to minimise the area occupied and their heating needs, arranging for controls to be correctly set, switching equipment off when it is not needed, and carefully considered draughtproofing to avoid excessive air infiltration (particularly in smaller churches, provided they are not damp)

- improving controls, particularly temperature and time controls and adding zone controls to avoid heating unused areas

- altering heating systems, particularly to improve efficiency and reduce fuel cost, and adding local systems where appropriate, perhaps sub-dividing the church by means of curtains, partitions and screens

- improving the insulation of the building, recognising that this is unlikely to be cost-effective in churches which are only heated once or twice a week or less.

Churches should consider giving one of their officers the task of energy management, monitoring fuel use and making sure that appropriate studies are undertaken, discussions held, and recommendations implemented. Specialist help can be obtained to set up appropriate systems. Since energy use ultimately results from what people require and how they behave, full discussion and publicity of energy matters are essential.

The Government's Environment and Energy Management Directorate (EEMD) provides information and sometimes financial and technical assistance on energy efficiency measures. Since these are constantly changing, details must be sought direct. If consultants are used, they will do the best job if good background material on the building, its heating system, typical temperatures and hours of use, and past fuel bills, is made available.

Church energy surveys reveal a number of recurrent causes of energy waste:

- **Poor operating practice** Nobody is responsible or quite understands what the system is supposed to do. Since there are usually no instructions, a rich folklore has developed about what is best. Each fuel bill is monitored only in horror and nothing positive is done.

- **Poor maintenance** A maintenance contract may have been placed with a company which has not done a thorough job, possibly because selection was entirely on price and against no specification, and the church has taken no interest in their visits and performance.

- **Crude controls** Many systems have only an on-off switch and perhaps a high limit thermostat. Investment in better time and temperature controls, and instruction in their use, will usually be quickly repaid on all but the fastest-responding local systems.

- **Controls not effective** as they are badly set, poorly selected, difficult to understand, badly located and without clear instructions. More than half the time switches the authors have seen in churches are either unused or not fully exploited for these reasons. Often no-one is sufficiently interested to overcome these problems without outside encouragement.

- **Excessive area heated** particularly where a number of spaces are on the same central system. Zone controls or local auxiliary heating should be considered.

- **Excessive heat output** in places. Thermostats may be insufficiently accurate or have failed or been tampered with. With central heating, the church may be cold while some adjacent rooms (passages, WCs, vestry, church hall) are too warm. Thermostatic radiator valves may be added to reduce local output; settings may be secured by fitting tamperproof guards.

- **Hot water** Large and occasionally uninsulated tanks may be heated continuously to unnecessarily high temperatures to satisfy infrequent demands, and circulating pipes may also be kept hot. The heat may be provided very inefficiently during the summer by a central heating boiler vastly over-sized for the duty and which could otherwise be switched off.

- **Central heating system losses** Equipment in the boiler room and pipes and ducts which do not contribute usefully to space heating should be well-insulated. Sluggish circulation should be improved by upgrading or adding pumps.

- **Low boiler efficiencies** particularly with older, oil-fired boilers. A dirty or badly-adjusted boiler can easily consume 20-30% more fuel than it ought to. Once the equipment has been cleaned and readjusted, if the test efficiency is much under 75% there may be good reasons for considering replacement. Substantial energy and money savings will often result from replacement by modern equipment. The number and size of boilers should be reviewed at the same time. If oil boilers are converted to gas-firing efficiencies sometimes drop; chimneys will often need lining and good technical advice should be obtained.

- **Undersized heat emitters** requiring needlessly long heating periods. A sound system may be extended or retained as background to a supplementary local or fast-responding system.

- **Inappropriate frost protection** arrangements and settings on wet central heating systems.

8.5 Destratification fans

Certain heating systems are prone to stratification with very hot air at high level. This is most likely with warm air and convective heating and in modern, lighter weight churches.

If stratification occurs – and one should always first measure what is actually happening – then destratification fans can be considered: see figure 6.4. Noise is rarely a problem with these fans, although there can be some 'drumming' if they are mounted on a lightweight ceiling and operate with certain types of speed-reducing equipment.

There is also the danger that the fans will cause uncomfortable draughts which negate their effect. Where they have been fitted, some users run the fans only during the warm–up period and switch them off when the church is occupied.

9

System selection and installation

In addition to the required temperature standards, criteria for selecting a heating system should include controls, running cost, options for future change and preservation of the building. It is impossible to give prescriptive solutions: professional advice will often be necessary. Measurement of temperatures and relative humidities gives a valuable check on performance and on possible risks to the fabric and contents. Monitoring should desirably take place for at least a year before and after any changes to the heating.

It is all too easy to make a poor choice when installing or replacing heating equipment. The obvious solutions may not be the right ones. Associated issues also need to be addressed, as suggested in figure 9.1. If the existing heating system, or parts of it, are in reasonable condition, one may be able to improve its efficiency, upgrade controls, or add more heat emitters. This chapter covers new systems, and the replacement or major upgrading of existing ones.

The starting point, whether for a historic church or a new building, should be to review the requirements against a checklist, as in figure 9.2. This will help to identify suitable and unsuitable methods, and possible problem areas.

Having gone through the needs systematically, the Parochial Church Council or other body or group will then be in a stronger position to begin the process of preparing a brief.

9.1   Stating the requirements

A clear brief will often need to incorporate requirements for preservation, ventilation and humidity control, in addition to heating itself. Additional specialist advice will often be required since heating consultants and contractors will not necessarily be aware of special features of the building and its contents which might be indirectly affected for better or worse by the heating. The specialists should also be asked to comment on the proposals.

Fig. 9.1   Problems and associated issues

Problem	Initial reaction	Associated issues
The boiler is elderly or broken down.	Replace the boiler with a similar one.	Is the present size of boiler likely to be adequate throughout its life of perhaps 20 years? It may be too big or too small. Review boiler type and fuel supply. Is this sort of heating required now?
The church is cold.	Add more heat, more radiators, additional heaters, a larger boiler.	Is the basic heating system adequate? Would alterations to the building improve the situation? Are the controls adequate and properly used?
The heating costs too much to run.	The church needs to be insulated and draughtproofed, the hours of heating operation restricted, and a cheaper fuel used.	Is the system well-maintained and operating efficiently? Is the basic method of heating right for the particular church and its particular usage? Would the mission of the church be helped by spending *more* on the heating to make the premises more comfortable?
A new church is being built.	It should be well centrally heated.	How is the building likely to be used? Is central heating the most appropriate? What running costs can be expected (clients often give this little priority until they get the first fuel bills)? What measures can be taken to minimise energy requirements?

The brief should state:

- the areas to be included in the project, with typical uses, times of use, and the comfort conditions required during those times

- any temperature, humidity and air quality requirements necessary for the preservation of the building and its contents

- physical and aesthetic constraints on the installation

- any relevant technical requirements and standards

- where appropriate, any requirements for investigating re-use of the existing system

- general intentions regarding operation (and responsibilities for operation), control and maintenance

- the relative importance of capital and running costs

- requirements for future flexibility in extent of system, patterns of use, furnishing arrangements, fuel choice, and proposed alterations and extensions to the buildings

- procedures and precautions to be followed during the installation work

- requirements for monitoring before and after installation.

The brief should also include relevant background information (e.g. plans, sections, specifications, mechanical and electrical drawings, main supply capacities, studies previously undertaken), or at least a guide to what exists and where it can be found.

The brief should be widely discussed in order to reach a balanced view and to make sure that all concerned appreciate what is to be done. Otherwise too much may be expected: living room conditions with the stability of a museum at minimum running cost!

Fig. 9.2   Check list

1. Check supply capacities for water, gas, electricity.	If oil, solid fuel or LPG are considered, discuss supply, price, storage and access with potential suppliers.
2. For each area establish: minimum temperature, minimum fresh air requirement, appropriate humidity levels, system response rate.	Expert advice may be required.
3. Is low maintenance equipment required (this may incur additional capital cost)?	Review maintenance requirements, frequency and cost. Consider availability of suitable con-tractors. Make installer responsible for all maintenance for the first year after installation.
4. Is equipment accessible for maintenance?	Can it be relocated?
5. Can the premises be zoned, now or in the future?	Zoning can reduce energy consumption by only heating the areas required.
6. Is heating required in any unoccupied areas to prevent moisture migration?	Unheated rooms (vestries, tower base, stores) can become damper when other parts are better heated, particularly with pressurised warm air heating.
7. Is the roof high (over 6–7m)?	Choose heating systems which minimise stratification. Radiant heating component may be useful to increase human comfort.
8. How important is uniformity of heat distribution? What is maximum temperature range acceptable?	Consider range of possible uses.
9. Is condensation protection required?	Achievable either by maintaining minimum temperature level or maximum humidity level. Dehumidification can sometimes be an energy-efficient option.
10. Are there any artefacts (organs, wall paintings, pictures, etc.) requiring tight environmental limits?	It may be possible to provide localised protection or control. Some artefacts may be susceptible to trace element pollution.
11. What type of roof(s) does the building have?	Lead roofs without intervening ventilated air spaces in particular may be susceptible to con-densation and corrosion.
12. What is the current and projected use of the premises?	Regular and frequent use may have different optimum solutions from sporadic or intermittent use.

13. Are different types of activity undertaken in different areas, or in the same area?	Different temperature levels may need to be available at different times in some areas.
14. What noise level limits are appropriate?	Noise levels for worship need to be lower than for some other activities. Special requirements may be necessary for public music performance, particularly if recording or broadcasting. There may also be external noise from fresh air intakes to warm air heaters.
15. What types of control are needed?	Tamperproof, or automatically resetting, controls are essential in publicly accessible areas.
16. What regular control adjustments are required, and who will make them and where?	Ensure that systems specified are in the right place and can be understood by those who will operate and maintain them.
17. What guidelines are offered by the Diocesan Advisory Committee?	Remember you will need a faculty. Many DACs have their own preferred methods and may discourage certain types of heating.
18. Are there any particular insurance requirements or constraints?	Consult the church's insurance company.
19. Is the building listed, grant-aided by English Heritage, or in a Conservation Area?	Make contact with the appropriate authorities.

9.2   The heating consultant

A heating consultant is recommended, preferably for a full design and contract supervision service, but at least to help define the problems, review statutory and insurance requirements, establish a performance specification, and comment on contractors' proposals and workmanship. Names may be sought from the Diocesan Advisory Committee Secretary, or from the church's architect/surveyor. In order to benefit from feedback it may be helpful to identify suitable individuals or firms in an area and to retain them for advice on a number of churches over a period.

One may be tempted to rely on heating suppliers and installers and save the cost of a consultant. This is sometimes appropriate if the requirements are clear, simple, and specific. However, it can be impossible to judge between apples and oranges in different suppliers' speculative schemes, which may also employ a limited range of equipment. Without a proper specification, there is little incentive for the supplier to attend to finer details such as minimum running cost, intelligibility to the user, flexibility in operation, and response to future change, let alone the possible impact of changed environmental conditions on the fabric of a historic church. While these would improve performance and appearance, if prices are not evaluated against a common specification, their inclusion could well lose the bidder the job by increasing their tender price! Many suppliers offer minimal or inappropriate controls with their systems and may not appreciate that operating regimes and requirements for churches are different from domestic and commercial needs. A few unscrupulous salesmen even browbeat vicars into buying equipment on the basis of claimed capital or fuel cost savings and dismiss legitimate concerns about possible adverse effects.

9.3   System selection

Selection must be made carefully by the client with their architect/surveyor and heating consultant. Difficult decisions should not be assigned to those who may not see the whole picture. Before a scheme is finalised, it should be discussed carefully with those who will operate and maintain it; they will often have valuable insights into details of design, specification, installation and operation.

Figure 9.3 gives brief details of the major heating systems to assist in selection. The following points should also be borne in mind:

● local heating is generally more energy-efficient than overall space heating, particularly for occasional needs

● operation should be very carefully considered, and controls selected and sited accordingly

● if the existing heating lacks capacity but is in good order, it may be worth supplementing it rather than replacing it entirely; it may be able to provide conservation or background heating to the advantage of the building, with a new supplementary system to create the desired comfort conditions.

Although each building and its requirements must be considered individually, certain situations recur. Solutions depend very much on the size of the church, its intensity of use, whether other facilities are combined with it, fuel availability and cost. Simply, in an occasionally used church, one does not want to waste a lot of heat warming the fabric excessively, and radiant and air heating will be the most effective, with suitable background conservation heating where necessary. With more continuous use, the fabric will inevitably be warmed and so there is a wider range of heating options, though one should avoid systems involving high air temperatures and too much ventilation, which will be expensive to run and make the church too dry in cold weather.

Fig. 9.3   System selection

Heater type	Efficiency	Controls	Applications
Gas convector heaters	Typically 75-85%.	Individual thermostatic, or central. Can be grouped.	Smaller churches. Down-blow fanned units with bottom outlets can work well.
Low temperature hot water radiator systems (LTHW)	Variable. New boiler typically 80% efficient. Condensing boilers up to 90%. However system losses may reduce efficiencies.	Many different systems available. Good control design essential to achieving energy efficiency.	More regular heating patterns. Comparatively small individual volumes to be heated (see also LTHW system with fan convectors).
LTHW system with fan convectors	As above.	As above.	Larger spaces. Faster response.
Electric storage heaters	Up to 95% of delivered energy (30-35% including electricity production efficiency losses).	Units usually have inbuilt thermostat. Units available with automatic charge controls, governed by outside weather.	Where gas not available. Regular use. Small churches. Conservation heating. Background heating (with alternative system to provide comfort).
Electric panel heaters and tubular heaters	100% of delivered energy (30-35% including electricity production efficiency losses).	Individual thermostatic control. Can have individual clocks and can use remote signalling. Local 'on-demand' timers useful.	Small rooms in well insulated buildings. 'Topping-up' for other systems. Can also use overnight rate for conservation heating in heavy buildings.
Gas-fired overhead radiant tubes	75-90%.	Normally on/off control, but may have modulating control.	Spot heating. High roof buildings (>4.5m). (Unflued systems only in areas where humidity is not a problem).
Floor-standing warm air heaters	75-80% (flued), over 90% (unflued gas only).	Thermostatically controlled. On/off, High/med/low, or modulating burners.	Seldom appropriate.
Gas-fired pressurised air systems	Indirect (flued): 75-80%. Direct (unflued): over 90%.	Thermostatically controlled. On/off, High/med/low, or modulating burners.	Large spaces without subdivision. Intermittent usage. Building needs to be relatively airtight.
Electric radiant heaters	100% of delivered energy (30-35% after generation losses).	Normally on/off but some are variable. Local 'on-demand' timers useful.	Large spaces with intermittent use. Mounting height up to 4m.

Advantages	Disadvantages
Easy to install. High efficiency. Cost effective, especially for small areas. Low running costs. Good for zoning.	Units are bulky compared with radiators. Limited by flue outlets through external walls. Flue terminals outside may be visually or structurally unacceptable. High surface temperatures with natural convectors. Stratification likely with natural convectors; fan-assisted better. Each heater needs annual servicing.
Centralised plant/flue and control. Proven technology. Flexible layouts. Emitters small compared with other systems. Low running costs (with proper plant and controls). Good temperature control possible. Easy to zone. Choice of fuel.	Labour intensive installation. Risk of freezing/flooding. Needs separate plant space. Higher capital cost than other systems. Boiler needs servicing once/twice per year; yearly inspection of all associated plant. Cleaning flues and chimneys.
As above, but gives more rapid warm-up. Lower installation cost than radiators. Needs less wall space than radiators.	As above. Individual emitters may be bulky. Can be noisy at high speed. Consider high speed for warm-up and low speed during the service. More maintenance required.
Simple to install. Low capital cost. Useful for conservation heating. Minimal servicing, but fanned versions may need fan inspection.	Often relatively high running costs. Large unit size. May be less effective at end of day (e.g. for evening meetings). Need robust electrical supply. Fire risk. Inflexible operation.
Simple to install. Low capital cost. Small units. Fast responding. No maintenance.	Very high fuel costs may lead to high running costs if not used sparingly. Need robust electrical supply. Fire risk, need effective overheat protection.
Needs no floor space. Efficient. Rapid warm-up. Lower air temperature for same comfort level. No air movement.	May be noisy. Poor maintenance access. May produce uncomfortable conditions. May cause discolouration. Often obtrusive visually. Servicing once/twice per year (access at high level may be difficult).
Low capital/installation cost.	Unflued versions generally not suitable in churches. Often gives stratification. Takes up floor space. Frequently noisy and visually unattractive. Servicing once/twice per year.
Low capital/installation cost. Overcomes draught problems. Rapid warm-up. Good heat distribution from a small number of outlets (often just one).	Needs effective sound attenuation inside the church and for air intake. Moisture and trace elements may cause damage with direct systems. Condensation may occur, particularly in hidden spaces. Indirect systems may produce too dry an atmosphere. May give rise to stratification if air temperatures too high or velocities too low. Rapid fluctuations may be unsuitable for conservation. Servicing once/twice per year.
Rapid warm-up. Heat people directly. Flexible and small. Cheap to install. Good for intermittent use. Minimal maintenance.	Use standard rate electricity. Appearance/colour of light. Running costs may be high. Fire risk. Element life.

Whatever the size and occupancy, it is vital that the heating and ventilation help to protect the church and its contents as far as possible from decay. Normally, the requirements are for adequate ventilation or dehumidification to avoid sustained condensation and remove excess moisture, and for sufficient heating to keep all vulnerable surfaces sufficiently above the dew point temperature of the air. Closer control may be necessary where there are valuable items to be preserved. Much depends on the associated ventilation. It will often be enough to ensure a small through-draught at all times and to make someone responsible for opening a larger number of ventilators once a week, preferably after the most intensive period of occupancy. In fine, dry weather the building can be further warmed and excess moisture removed by leaving the doors and windows open for longer periods, but not in humid weather or overnight when the temperature falls and the relative humidity rises.

To determine whether ventilation rates are appropriate, a thermohygrograph should be placed in the church and the degree and method of ventilation varied. It should soon become clear what is having a significant effect on relative humidities.

If it is difficult to find people to adjust the ventilation, then automatic control of fans, ventilators or dehumidifiers should be considered. The effectiveness of these will normally be greater, and the overall cost less, than the consequences of either ignoring the problem or attempting to solve it by heating alone.

9.4   Some installation requirements

In the Church of England new heating systems, and alterations to existing systems, will require the authority of a faculty. Plans and specifications should be submitted to the Diocesan Advisory Committee for consideration, and the DAC's advice should be sought at an early stage for any sizeable or controversial proposals.

Associated building work may cost as much as the heating itself, and the choice of system will often be influenced by the need to keep this to a minimum. Great care is required, something which firms and operatives without long experience of church work may not appreciate.

In order to minimise disruption and possible damage, good use should be made of existing facilities (such as Victorian floor ducts) in a new installation, and any cutting into the building should be minimised. A badly located item can always be repositioned; something wrongly cut out may be lost for ever. Any boring or cutting-out should always be carefully set out in advance, under architectural supervision, and the work done by the appropriate craftsman, not by the pipe fitter. The progress of all cutting should be carefully monitored: for instance, walls thought to be solid may turn out to be rubble-filled. Small test holes should be made first if there is any uncertainty. Permissible drilling and cutting techniques should be carefully specified: modern vibratory tools can weaken the structure and loose materials may fall away.

In historic buildings, the following guidelines should always be followed:

- chases should not be made in brickwork, masonry or plaster without the consent of the architect

- holes or chases should not be made in or through buttresses, piers, mullions, columns, detached shafts or vaulting ribs without the consent of the architect

- no holes should be drilled in, or fixings made to bosses, unless they have already been drilled for a previous installation

- pipes should not be laid over the surface of carvings, paintings or mouldings

- pipes and heat emitters should not normally be run below historic artefacts, in particular paintings and wall paintings

- holes should be as small as possible, carefully drilled and inconspicuously located

- all brackets and fixings should be as small as practicable

- moisture and corrosion-resistant materials should always be used for exterior work, and preferably throughout

- before any work is started the heating contractor should submit proposals for the routes of all pipes and cables and the precise locations of all items of equipment. Typical details of holes and fixings should also be submitted, with samples where necessary. All routes and positions and any alterations to the drawn scheme should be agreed on site and in writing before any work commences

- hot work permits must be issued where gas torches or burners are to be used and the specified safety practices followed; where possible this type of work should be pre-fabricated off-site.

Heaters and pipework should be selected and located to avoid staining surfaces and decorations. The following guidelines should be followed:

- radiators and other high temperature heat sources fixed close to walls cause bad stains. A projecting shelf above helps, but to be effective it must also project at least 150 mm at either side, turn down a similar amount at the ends and be well sealed to the wall at the back.

- natural convectors with top discharge give similar problems. Front discharge units and skirting convectors are preferable, or the units should be spaced 100 mm or more away from the wall. Convectors and heaters against walls should be sealed at the back, or to a flat backing board if the wall is uneven.

- fan convectors and forced warm air systems give little trouble except where wall grilles are set flush and the system remains warm while the fan is off. Grilles should be well sealed round the edge or streaks may appear. Flush grilles should never be used with gravity warm air systems as they cause bad stains.

- pipes and electric tubular heaters cause troublesome staining if less than about 40 mm from the wall and at brackets; floor stands are best, otherwise insulated brackets should be used or the pipes encased.

- pattern staining may occur where some parts of a surface are colder than others, as with plaster ceilings on wooden joists. The effect is particularly noticeable where the surface is swept by air currents from convector heaters and large column radiators. Problems may be minimised by insulation above or by using different heaters.

It is essential to obtain 'as-fitted' drawings of the system (preferably with a framed schematic fixed to the wall), a record of all items of equipment and their maintenance requirements, commissioning records, and clear operating and maintenance instructions for the entire system. There should also be simple instructions on the use of the controls, records of their preferred settings, and a fault-finding procedure for the non-specialist. It can be difficult to get satisfactory material from contractors, and assistance from the architect/surveyor and the heating consultant will often be necessary to ensure that the information is of the right quality, and that any consequential problems which might arise from incorrect use of the system are identified where possible. Three copies should normally be requested, one for filing, one available in the church, and one for the church safe in case the others are lost.

If the fabric of the building is to be altered, the following priority list for reducing heating requirements is common:

- insulation over existing ceilings, detailed to avoid condensation problems; voids should be inspected regularly for a year or two after insulation, preferably in cold weather and at times of high RH in the church, to be sure that all is well

- in suitable circumstances, and with due regard to acoustics, the church may be subdivided to reduce the heated volume

- where the church is heated for several days at a time, insulating fills may be considered for cavity walls in good condition in sheltered locations

- double glazing in unusual circumstances, e.g. to reduce bad downdraughts or to protect vulnerable stained glass windows, for which external secondary glazing is often the most effective, where visually acceptable.

For churches in intermittent use, the payback periods for these measures will often be far longer than the five year maximum commonly used commercially. The work may nevertheless be justified by the long life of a church and if funds are raised by separate appeal.

9.5 Flue and chimney installation

Flues often give technical and aesthetic problems. They need to be matched to the appliance and to comply with Building Regulations and the Clean Air Act. However, where an old system is replaced by one of equivalent power, detailed compliance with current Acts may not be necessary.

Larger boilers require substantial flues which can be difficult to accommodate. Existing flues will not necessarily be suitable, since:

- the path may be tortuous; it may have relied on continuous heat from a coal-fired appliance to work satisfactorily

- the lining will often have failed

- the area may be inadequate for more powerful equipment

- condensation of water vapour from gas and combustion products from oil may not only damage the flue but soak through to external surfaces of the chimney, bringing with it sulphates and tars from earlier coal-firing, sometimes with disastrous results

- where flue gas temperatures are increased, the flue may fail and ignite nearby timbers or inflammable materials deposited in the roof space e.g. by birds

- satisfactory cleaning arrangements may be difficult to organise.

The re-use of an existing flue requires a thorough survey. Sharp bends may have to be eased, and replacement or re-lining may be necessary. For gas and some oil-fired equipment it may be possible to use a flexible stainless steel flue liner. A properly-lined flue of insufficient capacity for atmospheric combustion may be adequate for pressurised burners, or with fan assistance. Older flues usually have a large thermal capacity and may not function correctly under natural draught until thoroughly warm. This may never occur if heating operates intermittently, exacerbating condensation and sooting problems. Where flues are not suitably lined, particularly for gas boilers, chemicals from the previous oil and coal combustion may work through to the face, damaging masonry and plasterwork. Prefabricated insulated flues, often in stainless steel, are now widely used for new installations. Balanced and dilution flues for gas and some small oil boilers have been discussed earlier (see section 4.6).

Flues and chimneys for condensing boilers need to be drained. Depending on boiler and chimney design, this can sometimes be back into the boiler but independent drainage may be required.

Conclusion

There is no point in making the church comfortable and reducing fuel costs if the process causes damage to the building and its contents. It is best to set down the specific requirements and the things that are likely to need monitoring on a regular or occasional basis. The situation should then be reviewed formally from time to time, using instrumentation where necessary, particularly before and after making potentially significant alterations.

Many churches that wish to improve their heating have already stood for centuries, much of that time without any sort of heating. Few manufacturers of heating systems would expect their products to last for more than a few decades so that each installation represents only a minor event in the history of the building. It is important to intervene as little as possible whilst rendering the buildings useful to serve the present age.

Further reading

Bemrose, C.R. and Smith, I.E., *Thermal stratification in intermittently heated heavyweight buildings (Churches)*, Building Serv. Eng. Res. Technol., 13(3), (1992) pp 119-131

Bordass, W.T., *Pressurised direct gas-fired heating*, Church Building 22-23 (Autumn 1993)

British Gas, *Direct Gas-fired Heating at the Church of St Cross, Winchester*, British Gas (1990)

Building Research Establishment Digests 180 (1975), 270 (1983), 369 (1992) and British Standards 5250 (1989) and 6229 (1982), *Condensation*

Building Research Establishment, *Thermal Insulation: Avoiding Risks*, HMSO (1994)

Burman, P. (ed.), *Treasures on Earth*, Donhead Publishing (1994)

Chartered Institution of Building Services, *CIBSE Guide, Section A* (current version in 10 parts), *CIBSE Energy Code* (current version)

Chartered Institution of Building Services, *Minimising the risk of legionnaires' disease*, Technical Memorandum 13 (1991)

Department of the Environment, *Degree Days*, Fuel Efficiency Booklet No. 7

Department of the Environment, *Introduction to Energy Efficiency in Museums, Galleries, Libraries and Churches*, Energy Efficiency Office, London (March 1994)

The Gas Council, *Notes for Guidance on the Installation of Flueless Gas Appliances for Church Heating*, Watson House Bulletin Statement, (1957)

International Institute for Conservation, *Conservation Within Historic Buildings*, Vienna Congress (1980)

Kerr, Jill, *The Repair and Maintenance of Glass in Churches*, Church House Publishing (1991)

Marks, B., *Heat and Light - a practical guide to energy conservation in church buildings*, St Andrew Press, Edinburgh (1994)

Martin, P.L. and Oughton, D.R., *Faber and Kell's Heating and Air Conditioning of Buildings* (8th edition), Butterworth (1994)

McIntyre, D.A., *Indoor Climate*, Applied Science Publishers (1980)

National Building Studies, *Condensation in Sheeted Roofs*, Research Paper No. 23, HMSO (1958)

Newton, R.G., *The Deterioration and Conservation of Painted Glass: A Critical Bibliography*, Oxford University Press (1982)

Thomson, G., *The Museum Environment* (2nd edition), Butterworth (1986)